Marriage and Mandatory Abortion among the 17th-century Siraya

John Robert Shepherd

American Ethnological Society Monograph Series, Number 6
Mary Moran, Series Editor

Library of Congress Cataloging-in-Publication Data
Marriage and Mandatory Abortion among the 17th-century Siraya / John Robert Shepherd
    p.cm. – (American Ethnological Society monograph series; no. 6)
    Includes bibliographical references.
    ISBN 0-913167-71-1
    1. Siraya (Taiwan people)–Marriage customs and rites–History–17th century.
    2. Abortion–Taiwan–History–17th century. 3. Marriage customs and rites–Taiwan–
    History–17th century. I. Title. II. Series.
DS799.43.S57S54   1995
304.6'67'0951249–dc20   95-15069

**Copies of this title and other titles from the American Anthropological Association
may be ordered from:**
American Anthropological Association
2200 Wilson Boulevard, Suite 600
Arlington, VA 22201
Telephone: 703.528.1902
Fax: 703.528.3546

http://www.aaanet.org/publications/Books-and-Monographs.cfm

Contents

Acknowledgments

The research reported here was supported during 1988 by an IUP-CSSC Language and Research Fellowship at the Inter-University Program in Taipei, Taiwan, and during 1989 by an ACLS-SSRC Fellowship in Chinese Studies. I also wish to thank the Institute of Ethnology, Academia Sinica, for hosting me as a visiting scholar during those years. Comments and assistance from Leonard Blusse, Ch'en Wen-te, Donald Donham, Tamara Hamlish, Barbara Harrell, Nancy Howell, Huang Hsuan-wei, Liu Pin-hsiung, Steven Sangren, and Margery Wolf are gratefully acknowledged. Earlier versions of various portions of this monograph have been presented to the Institute of Ethnology, Academia Sinica (1990), the Stanton Humanities Seminar at the California Institute of Technology (1990), the Department of Anthropology at the University of Virginia (1991), and the Conference on Matrilineality and Patrilineality at the University of Minnesota (1992), and I thank these institutions for those opportunities.

1

Introduction:
Sirayan Mandatory Abortion

In 1624 the Dutch East India Company (the "Company") established a colonial outpost on Taiwan (Formosa) that was to last until 1662.
From the island's best harbor at Tayouan (modern Tainan) the Company
hoped to conduct an intermediary trade between China and Japan. The
Company also hoped to profit from the export of the thousands of
deerskins produced by Taiwan's aboriginal hunters. In the vicinity of
Tayouan harbor, these headhunting hunter-horticulturalists lived in
large, densely populated villages that were in a constant state of war
with one another. Today these Austronesian people are classified as
belonging to an ethnolinguistic group called Siraya (see Figure 1).[1]

In July 1627 the Reverend Georgius Candidius arrived in Taiwan
and shortly thereafter took up residence in the Sirayan village of Sinkan,
which lay a few miles inland from Tayouan harbor. The village council
of Sinkan welcomed Candidius in the expectation that his presence in
the village would bring Dutch military assistance should the village be
attacked by one of its many traditional enemies (Blusse 1984:164). Because the Company lacked the resources to extend political control
beyond its coastal entrepot in Tayouan until 1635, it depended on
Candidius for political intelligence regarding developments among the
villages in the colony's hinterland. Candidius, in turn, used his reports
to call upon the Company for greater support of his mission work
(Campbell 1903:89-100; Blusse 1984). So it was with great seriousness of
purpose that Candidius wrote his famous ethnographic description of
the Siraya, entitled "Account of the Inhabitants" (hereafter "Account"),
in December 1628, after nearly 16 months of residence in Sinkan.[2]

One passage of Candidius's Account has shocked and perplexed all
subsequent readers; this is his description of Sirayan mandatory abortion:

> In the first years of marriage the wife has no children; for, according to the
> laws and customs of this people, a woman is not allowed to bear children
> till she is thirty-five, thirty-six, or thirty-seven, years of age; for, when she
> is with child, the fruit of her womb is destroyed. This is brought about in
> the following way: They call one of their priestesses, and, on her arrival, the
> woman lies down on a couch or on the floor, and is then pushed, pinched,

1

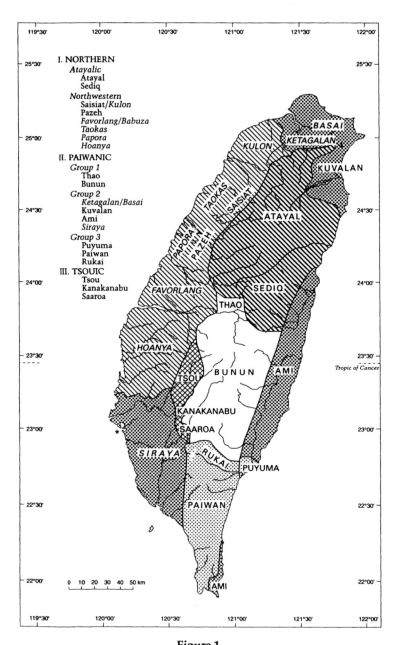

Figure 1.
Aboriginal Ethnolinguistic Groups of Taiwan. Italics indicate extinct languages. * indicates the location of Tayouan harbor. Reprinted from Shepherd 1993:31, with the permission of Stanford University Press. ©1993 by the Board of Trustees of the Leland Stanford Junior University.

and roughly handled till abortion follows, which occasions more pain than if the child had been brought living into the world. It is not for lack of maternal love among these women that this system is followed, but because their priestesses teach them so to act. It would be considered a great shame, a great sin, if women bore any children before the age mentioned above, and thus the fruit of their wombs is generally destroyed. They themselves have often confessed to me that they have been with child fifteen or sixteen times and had practised abortion each time. One woman told me that she was with child the seventeenth time, but would now be allowed to bring her child into the world and to be born in the natural way; so that it is only when women are about thirty-seven to thirty-eight years of age and are with child that they allow their children to see the light of day without practising the sin of abortion. [Campbell 1903:19–20]

Thus Candidius reports that Sirayan priestesses forced young married women to induce miscarriages and terminate all their pregnancies. Note that the rule applies to wives and that this is not a custom directed at pregnant but unmarried women. Only when wives reached their mid-thirties did Sirayan custom allow them to give live birth. Several brief reports by Dutch observers other than Candidius (cited throughout this monograph) corroborate Candidius' report and confirm that the Siraya practiced mandatory abortion (and perhaps some infanticide as well).[3]

Mandatory abortion of all pregnancies until a woman reaches her mid-thirties is both unusual and extreme, as such customs go in world ethnography.[4] Over the centuries Sirayan mandatory abortion has attracted the attention of commentators ranging from Montesquieu and Malthus to the ethnopsychiatrist Devereux. These commentators have proposed a variety of explanations for Sirayan mandatory abortion ranging from the demographic to the Freudian. None, however, attempts seriously to demonstrate his explanation or to analyze Sirayan history, institutions, or culture. Sirayan mandatory abortion presents us with an ethnographic puzzle against which we may test a variety of the explanatory paradigms current in anthropology and history. In this monograph I use the case of Sirayan mandatory abortion to test the adequacy of the interpretations proposed to date and on that basis to propose some of my own.

Through a reconstruction of traditional Sirayan society and culture, this monograph attempts to locate and explicate the meaning of Sirayan mandatory abortion. I shall argue that in organizing their society around male age grades and matrifocal households, the Siraya delayed the creation of conjugal families until relatively late in the life cycles of Sirayan men and women.[5] Mandatory abortion provided the means by which this delay was achieved. The Siraya themselves appear to have understood mandatory abortion as necessary to avoid the supernatural danger to headhunters caused by the pregnancy of headhunters' wives.

Both the practice of massage abortion and beliefs that pregnancy creates a mystical link between wives and husbands that endangers headhunting are widespread among Austronesian cultures (see Chapter 5). Seventeenth-century Siraya institutions of mandatory abortion and separate (duolocal) residence after marriage (that radically delayed the formation of conjugal families) represent an extreme development of these widespread Austronesian patterns. But before I elaborate my argument I want to review and evaluate the ability of demographic and cultural materialist explanations to account for Sirayan mandatory abortion. I shall also suggest how feminist and symbolic schemes of anthropological analysis can enrich our understanding of the Siraya, but only after the institutional pattern of Sirayan marriage has been understood.

Candidius's Account and his depiction of the Sirayan practice of abortion have attracted scholarly attention since the Account was first published. This monograph thus falls within a long tradition of commentary, though analysis here is supplemented by the reports from the 1623 reconnoitering of a Siraya village for the Company by Jacob Constant and Barent Pessaert (Blusse and Roessingh 1984), the Dutch village censuses (Nakamura 1936, 1937; Shepherd 1993:38–46), and the description of Siraya religious practices by David Wright published in 1671 (Wright 1671, reprinted in Shepherd 1986). Candidius's Account nevertheless remains the classic source on the 17th-century Siraya, and my analysis must, therefore, provide a close reading of the Account, integrate Candidius's and others' observations into a coherent pattern, and reconcile this with modern anthropological learning. The analysis must also be capable of accounting for the historical response of the Siraya to Dutch attempts to abolish mandatory abortion. I shall make particular use of comparisons between the Siraya and cognate groups of Formosan aborigines, especially the Ami, who have been the subject of several modern studies. Comparisons between the Ami and the Siraya are appropriate, as the close relationship between the Ami and Sirayan languages and the similarities in the institutions of the two groups have long been recognized (Ferrell 1969; Wang Sung-hsing 1964).[6]

Before proceeding further I need to dispel skepticism that massage abortion (in the absence of modern medicine) could have been practiced so widely without seriously damaging the health and fertility of Sirayan women. Modern wisdom assumes that nonmedical abortions are as likely to kill the mother as the fetus.[7] Yet Candidius, though he reports that abortion caused severe pain for Sirayan women, never suggests that the women's lives were thereby endangered, nor does he or any other Dutch author note any shortage of adult females in the Sirayan population that might have been caused by abortion-related deaths. In fact, massage abortion was probably the safest of the premodern/prescientific methods of inducing abortion.

Two recent studies of traditional abortion practices, one from Thailand and one from the Philippines, provide detailed descriptions of masssage abortion (Narkavonnakit and Bennett 1981:60–61 and Gallen 1982:39; see also International Fertility Research Program 1981). The following account is drawn from these two studies.[8] To start the procedure the pregnant woman lies on her back. The practitioner begins by massaging the woman's stomach to loosen the muscles and locate the uterus. The practitioner then presses on and manipulates the uterus, stopping only when the woman complains of great pain. These sessions may be repeated at intervals, or over a number of days. The effect of the manipulation is to induce (painful) uterine contractions. These contractions cut off the circulation of blood through the placenta, thereby causing a demise of the fetus (cf. Taussig 1936:97, 127, 355). Within a week or two the woman experiences labor pains and a natural abortion occurs, resulting in the expulsion of the nonvital fetus.

External manipulation of the uterus, along with the uterus's own contractions, may also cause the partial dislodging of the placenta and result in bleeding; once the uterus has expelled the fetus and placenta, further contractions cause this bleeding to stop (cf. Potts et al. 1977:46). Complications from massage abortion are most likely to be caused by blood loss, or infection related to incomplete elimination of placental tissue. The studies from Thailand and the Philippines document that massage abortions do entail some risk but are less likely to give rise to complications than other traditional or nonhospital methods of abortion (Narkavonnakit and Bennett 1981:61; Gallen 1982:41). Most dangerous are traditional methods that involve inserting foreign objects into the cervix; these create a risk of serious infections that massage abortions avoid (Potts et al. 1977:181).[9] Massage abortions skillfully performed may well involve less danger to the mother's health than giving live birth.[10]

Most massage abortions appear to have been obtained by the end of the first trimester (Narkavonnakit and Bennett 1981:59, Gallen 1982:40). By the third month of pregnancy the uterus has expanded and risen from the pelvic to the abdominal region and has become more accessible (vulnerable) to massage. Aborting early in the pregnancy involves the expulsion of a smaller mass of tissue, a smaller placenta, less bleeding, and less risk to the woman (cf. Taussig 1936:136).

Massage abortion need have little adverse effect on a woman's subsequent ability to carry a fetus to term, and it involves less strain or trauma to the uterus than childbirth. Thus, repeated massage abortions, when skillfully performed, need not have had an adverse effect on Sirayan women's health and fertility.

Notes

1. The Siraya were only one of nearly two dozen Formosan aboriginal groups; for a more general account of the situation in 17th-century Taiwan, see Shepherd 1993. The term "aborigine" has traditionally been used in Western ethnography to refer to Taiwan's Austronesian inhabitants in contrast to the immigrant Han Chinese ("Taiwanese"). "Aborigine" is also the English translation adopted by Taiwan's pan-aborigine movement for the self-appellation *yüan chu min* (Hsieh Shih-chung 1987:139–140).

2. The formal title is "Discourse and short description of the island of Formosa, examined and described by the Reverend Georgius Candidius, servant of the Holy Gospel and propagator of the Christian Religion on the Island. Datum Sinckan, on the island Formosa, 27 December 1628" (Blusse and Roessingh 1984:79). The Account in English translation may be found in Campbell 1903:9–25. Blusse and Roessingh (1984:78) have corrected Campbell's translation. Lach and Van Kley's recent summary (1993:1797–1827) suffers from use of the uncorrected text as well as ignorance of anthropological studies of Taiwan. The names of the main Siraya villages discussed are given here in Dutch romanizations; the Chinese equivalents are as follows (with the Dutch version first): Sinkan, Hsin-kang; Soulang, Hsiao-lung; Mattau, Ma-tou; Bakloan, Mu-chia-liu-wan; Tevorang, Ta-wu-lung.

3. I adopt the phrase "mandatory abortion" from the anthropologist Ferrell (1971). Of the many passages from Dutch sources cited in this monograph, only two seem to refer to infanticide rather than abortion. The clearest instance comes from a 1642 report referring to the punishment of three persons "who had murdered some young children" (Campbell 1903:189); this translates a Dutch phrase "moorderyen aen d'cleene kinderkens" (Grothe 1886:215). The second possible instance is the report of the Constant and Pessaert expedition of 1623 where "they kill these children" translates a Dutch phrase "brengen se die om den hals" that suggests killing by breaking the neck, but this is a common phrase used metaphorically for killing (Blusse and Roessingh 1984:70). Passages referring to abortion use such phrases as "the fruit of her womb is destroyed" [dooden sij de vrucht in haer lichaem] (Grothe 1886:19; Campbell 1903:20) and "the women when pregnant should no longer practise abortion [press away their innocent children]" [vrouwen, swanger wesende, van het affperssen haerer onnosele kinderen] (Grothe 1886:163; Campbell 1903:162). Thus it seems the Siraya practised both abortion and infanticide, but the prominence given by Candidius to descriptions of the aborting process suggest it was the more prevalent of the two practices. I thank Leonard Blusse for his help in identifying the Dutch passages.

4. Devereux's review of reports of abortion from some 350 societies confirms that abortion is widely practiced in a great number of societies and that the Sirayan case is extreme in two regards. First, it is extreme in the number of abortions reported for individual women (Devereux 1976:25–26, 84). Second, Sirayan society is the only society Devereux unqualifiedly codes as giving unconditional approval to abortions (in fact, mandating abortions). Devereux

tentatively classifies seven other groups as giving unconditional approval to abortion. In four of these abortion was approved in response to disruptive contact with Western culture (e.g., Spanish oppression, loss of morale, cargo cult). One group approved abortion of children born to unwed mothers. Of the remaining two, the Atjeh are reported to approve frequent abortion in and outside of marriage, and the Chaco are reported to approve abortion by a woman seeking to postpone motherhood and abortion by a married woman of her first pregnancy (Devereux 1976:185, 202–203, 361–371).

5. I use the term "matrifocal" to indicate that at the core of the household is a set of mother-daughter-sister bonds (cf. Tanner 1974). I wish to avoid importing assumptions that reckoning of descent or ancestral worship is important, as might be implied if the term "matrilineal" were used to describe these Siraya households.

6. An alternative might be to dismiss Candidius's report of mandatory abortion as a fiction. But my study of 17th-century Taiwan has given me the highest regard for the reliability of Candidius's report. In nearly every particular it has proven consistent with other Dutch reports, and many of the seemingly unusual ethnographic details he reports have close parallels in the ethnography of Formosan aborigines and Austronesians beyond Taiwan. The seriousness of purpose for which the Account was intended also bolsters its credibility. There is no reason therefore to question the accuracy of Candidius' report of mandatory abortion.

7. Linda Gordon notes that the campaign to decriminalize abortion led to an exaggeration of the dangers of "nonmedical" abortions. This has reinforced the scientific prejudices against traditional practices propagated by the medical community in its drive to professionalize abortion (Gordon 1976:52–53, 59–60).

8. I thank Barbara Harrell for her assistance in understanding these reports from a medical point of view. I alone am responsible for the account provided in the text.

9. Of course in societies where abortion is condemned, women are prevented from acquiring and passing on knowledge of abortion techniques. In these circumstances desperate women often resort to crude methods, including forms of external trauma that involve high risk (see Devereux 1976: passim). Where the social environment was hospitable to massage abortion (as it was among the Siraya), practitioners could acquire the experience and skill that would diminish risk to the mother. Massage abortion is widely reported among Austronesian cultures; see Jenks 1905:60; Cole 1922:262; Quirino and Garcia 1958:413; Dozier 1966:88; King 1976:195; Yu and Liu 1980:135–139; Pedrosa 1983:19; Miyamoto 1988:33–34.

10. See Potts et al. 1977:188. In 1929 maternal mortality in the United States averaged 7 per 1000 live births, 6.3 for whites and 12 for nonwhites (Dunn 1949: xxxix).

2

European Exegeses:
Montesquieu and Malthus

Candidius' Account was translated and widely reprinted (often in corrupt form) in many of the collections of foreign travel accounts popular in 17th- and 18th-century Europe (Blusse and Roessingh 1984:63–64). In this form, the Sirayan custom of mandatory abortion attracted the attention of its two most famous commentators, Montesquieu and Malthus.[1]

Montesquieu reports the Sirayan practice of abortion in the 23rd book of *The Spirit of the Laws*. Chapter XVI, entitled "The concern of the Legislator in the propagation of the Species," compares the Chinese to the Siraya:

> What need is there of inducing men by laws to propagation, when a fruitful climate yields a sufficient number of inhabitants? Sometimes the climate is more favourable than the soil; the people multiply, and are destroyed by famine: this is the case of China. Hence a father sells his daughters, and exposes his children. . . .

> For the same reason, the religion of the isle of Formosa does not suffer the women to bring their children into the world, till they are thirty-five years of age: the priestess before this age, by bruising the belly, procures abortion. [Montesquieu 1758:119]

According to Montesquieu, both the Chinese and the Siraya inhabit rich environments where population increases naturally and there is no need to encourage humankind to reproduce. Rather, these societies are in danger of overreproducing and must find ways to limit population growth. In the Chinese case population repeatedly outgrows its resources, causing recurrent famines that force families to resort to infanticide in order to survive. In contrast to the Chinese, the religion of Sirayan priestesses mandates abortions for women until they reach age 35, thereby enabling the Siraya to avoid famines by taking a preventive approach to overpopulation. Note that both religion and the meaning of abortion for the Siraya are unproblematic for Montesquieu; for him Sirayan religion serves a purely instrumental function in prescribing abortion as a means of population control.[2]

Montesquieu is the first in a long tradition that accounts for Sirayan mandatory abortion as a means of population control. This is despite the fact that Candidius's Account in no way suggests this interpretation, for Candidius does not so much as imply that population control was a motive of Siraya abortion, let alone discuss or note any unusual demographic consequences.

Malthus's *An Essay on the Principle of Population* comes next in the tradition inaugurated by Montesquieu. In a chapter entitled "Of the Checks to Population in the Islands of the South Sea," (Book I, chapter v), the Reverend Malthus takes the Siraya as an example of a society practicing a form of primitive communism. Because the community at large, rather than individual sets of parents, bore the burden of supporting children, Sirayan parents could produce children free of all economic restraint. Malthus thus traces the danger of overpopulation among the Siraya to the institution of primitive communism, in contrast to Montesquieu who traced the danger of overpopulation to a favorable climate. What prevented overpopulation among the Siraya? Malthus concludes that the positive checks to population had little effect upon the Siraya. Neither the deprivations inflicted on the lower orders by class stratification nor the ravages of warfare and disease were sufficient to hold Sirayan population in check.[3] Nor was the preventive check of sexual abstinence a possible means of birth control among the Siraya, for according to Malthus, "we could not expect to find among savages in such climates any great degree of moral restraint" (1989:55–56). Malthus concludes that the only means of population control left to the Siraya was to mandate abortion.[4] Mandating abortion was necessary to solve the free rider problem arising in a "community of goods" where parents produced children for whom they did not bear economic responsibility.

Malthus, like Montesquieu, understands Sirayan mandatory abortion as intended to prevent overpopulation. But Montesquieu focuses on the role of the priestesses and Sirayan religion in legislating mandatory abortion and enforcing compliance therewith. Malthus, by contrast, picks up another piece of Candidius's Account to link the institution of mandatory abortion to the nature of Sirayan marriage. According to Malthus, Sirayan marriage institutions restricted the access of husbands to wives, who resided in (what he assumes to be) their fathers' houses:

> In the island of Formosa, it is said that the women were not allowed to bring children into the world before the age of thirty-five. If they were with child prior to that period, an abortion was effected by the priestess, and till the husband was forty years of age the wife continued to live in her father's house, and was only seen by stealth. [Malthus 1989:56]

For Malthus the need to limit population growth dictated both the Sirayan custom of mandatory abortion and the requirement that young husbands only visit their wives by stealth. It appears that Malthus thought of the Sirayan postponement of conjugal coresidence as a preventive check analogous to the role that late age at marriage played in the English marriage pattern (cf. MacFarlane 1986). We will discuss these unusual features of Sirayan marriage at length below.[5]

Although Candidius's Account gives no hint of this interpretation, both Montesquieu and Malthus understood Sirayan mandatory abortion as a policy intended to limit population growth. This demographic approach has its modern proponents in Ferrell and among the cultural materialists.

Notes

1. Perhaps the most infamous claimed use of Candidius's Account was by the impostor Psalmanaazaar, who published his fictitious *An Historical and Geographical Description of Formosa, an Island subject to the Emperor of Japan* in 1704 (for accounts of this episode see Foley 1968 and Needham 1985). Most scholarly commentators have accepted Psalmanaazaar's claim to have used Candidius, along with several other sources, in composing his fraudulent description (Psalmanaazaar 1704:xiv; Blusse and Roessingh 1984:63; cf. Needham 1985:94–95). In fact, comparison of the two works reveals that Psalmanaazaar took almost nothing from Candidius. Psalmanaazaar invented a kingdom while Candidius describes a society of headhunters that lacked even village chiefs. Candidius's report that wives were forced to abort all pregnancies until they reached their thirties was apparently too fantastic (or not fantastic enough) for Psalmanaazaar, who instead invented a religion that required the regular sacrifice of 20,000 hearts of children (especially boys) under nine years of age (Psalmanaazaar 1704:153–55). Extinction was prevented by allowing men in Psalmanaazaar's Formosa to have many wives, "that they may beget many Children every year; of whom some of the Sons are Sacrific'd, but the Daughters are all preserv'd for Matrimony," (Psalmanaazaar 1704:178–179). Psalmanaazaar further informs us that there is no such thing as the French-pox in Formosa "because they allow Polygamy and prohibit Adultery," (1704:228). By contrast, Candidius describes a society that was monogamous but rife with adultery and fornication, though he reports no syphilis. Because Psalmanaazaar has failed to use Candidius's Account to any extent, we must turn elsewhere to find examples of the early reaction to the Sirayan practice of abortion.

2. In a later passage, Montesquieu points to the unusual position of authority occupied by elderly women in Sirayan society by likening Sirayan priestesses to "legislators." This is an aspect of Sirayan society that I will be concerned to explicate below; see "Gendered Perspectives," in Chapter 6.

3. Malthus employed the Sirayan case and fear of overpopulation to argue against utopian notions of primitive communism:

it is mentioned that there is no difference of condition among these people, and that their wars are so bloodless that the death of a single person generally decides them. In a very healthy climate, where the habits of the people were favourable to population and a community of goods was established, as no individual would have reason to fear *particular poverty* from a large family, the government would be in a manner compelled to take upon itself the suppression of the population by law; and, as this would be the greatest violation of every natural feeling, there cannot be a more forcible argument against a community of goods. [Malthus 1989:57, emphasis in original]

Thus for Malthus the immorality and the "unnaturalness" of Sirayan mandatory abortion provided an argument against the communism that made abortion necessary.

4. Malthus does not consider the possibility of other forms of preventive check (e.g., contraception and infanticide) in his discussion of the Siraya.

5. Except for the fact that Sirayan families were matrifocal rather than patriarchal, and Sirayan marriage duo-uxorilocal, Malthus' understanding of the two stages of Sirayan marriage comes close to my own; see Chapter 4.

3
Demographic Perspectives

The Question of Population Pressure

Raleigh Ferrell, a leading anthropologist of aboriginal Taiwan, follows the intellectual tradition of Montesquieu and Malthus, when he speculates that the Sirayan custom of mandatory abortion was adopted to curb population growth that "had for some reason reached an undesirable peak ... possibly due to increased commercial opportunities" (Ferrell 1971:220).[1] Sirayan villages were indeed quite large and thus gave the impression of high population density. Sirayan villages had by far the largest average village size of any Formosan ethnic group covered by the Dutch village censuses. (The Siraya average of 900–1000 is three to four times that of the next largest average.) But because there were fewer Sirayan villages per unit of area, the large average village size does not translate into markedly higher population density for the Siraya when compared to that of other plains groups (Shepherd 1993:38–46). (See Table 1.)

The population density of the Siraya and of all aboriginal Taiwan was quite low. Based on the village census for 1650 and rough estimates of ethnic territories,[2] the population density of the Siraya was 5.2 persons per square kilometer, compared to an average of 3.4 persons per square kilometer for the other seven plains aborigine ethnolinguistic groups under Dutch control.[3] These densities are quite low, even when compared to other swidden cultivators in Southeast Asia. Studies of shifting cultivation in the Philippines, Borneo, and Indonesia have observed densities of more than 20 persons per square kilometer, and estimated that swidden systems have a maximum carrying capacity as high as 50 persons per square kilometer. Higher densities than this have been observed in New Guinea and Polynesia.[4]

The low population densities of the Siraya and other Formosan aboriginal groups in the 17th century thus give no support to arguments that use population pressure to explain mandatory abortion.[5] Indeed the low population density of the Siraya suggests that their "legislators" might well have been concerned to increase rather than limit their numbers.

Table 1.

Plains Aborigine Population by Ethnic Group, 1650. Plains aborigine villages are assigned to ethnic groups according to Chang Yao-ch'i 1951. Reprinted from Shepherd 1993:41 with the permission of Stanford University Press.©1993 by the Board of Trustees of the Leland Stanford Junior University.

Ethnic group	No. of villages	No. of households	Pop.	Area (km²)	Avg. village pop.	Density (pop./km²)	Avg. village area (km²)	Avg. household size
Kuvalan	45	2,272	9,670	739	215	13.1	16	4.3
Ketagalan[a]	37	1,741	6,972	1,929	188	3.6	52	4.0
Taokas	11	781	2,935	1,315	267	2.2	120	3.8
Papora	4	118	454	196	114	2.3	49	3.8
Pazeh	7	379	1,649	474	236	3.5	68	4.4
Favorlang (Babuza)	11	681	3,171	1,198	288	2.6	109	4.7
Hoanya	13	1,000	3,940	2,650	303	1.5	204	3.9
Non-Siraya subtotal	128	6,972	28,791	8,501	225	3.4	66	4.1
Siraya	21	3,866	19,172	3,684	913	5.2	175	5.0
Total	149	10,838	47,963	12,185	322	3.9	82	4.4

[a] Ketagalan includes the recently distinguished Basai and Kulon groups.

Nor do qualitative reports of the condition of the 17th-century Siraya population indicate that they were destitute, pushing the limits of the carrying capacity of their land, or anything of the sort that would indicate food shortages or overpopulation. On the contrary, the Dutch were impressed by the large expanse of fertile but idle land that they judged the Siraya too lazy to cultivate (Campbell 1903:9–12).

More importantly on this score, the Dutch were also impressed by huge numbers of deer in Taiwan and the abundance of venison in the Siraya diet (Candidius, in Campbell 1903:12). Deer hunting easily rivaled agriculture in its contributions to Siraya nutrition. Taiwan in the seventeenth century was literally teeming with deer. This is documented by the records of deerskin exports kept by the Dutch. For the 18 years between 1634 and 1660 for which we have records, a total of 1,179,454 deerskins were exported, for an annual average of 65,525 skins (Nakamura 1959; Shepherd 1993:74, 465).[6] Thus the hunting sector of the Siraya economy was supplying large quantities of animal protein to Sirayan diets.

Nutritionists consider animal protein in the diet to be important to building up disease resistance, especially cell-mediated immunity (Cohen 1989:58, 167; Lunn 1991), and to reducing nutritional stress during growth. So we should not be surprised to learn that the Dutch admired the healthy bodies and tall stature of the Siraya. In 1623 the Dutch reported that Sirayan men were "on the average taller by a head and neck than our average man" (Blusse and Roessingh 1984:74). John Struys reported in the account of his visit to Taiwan in 1650 that "[t]he men are mostly well-bodied and lusty, especially those in the valleys and plain country, those living in the mountain regions being rather smaller and less robust" (Campbell 1903:255). Recent work by historical demographers demonstrates that height can be a reliable indicator of nutrition, health, and life expectancy (Floud et al. 1990). These reports of relative stature provide us with valuable evidence of the good health and nutrition of the 17th-century Siraya.[7]

Thus the qualitative evidence on Siraya conditions of life gives us no reason to accept an argument that sees mandatory abortion as an adaptation to overpopulation. There are yet other points to be made in this regard.[8] When the Dutch missionaries pressed for the abolition of mandatory abortion in Siraya villages, fears of overpopulation were never expressed in opposition, nor was overpopulation ever noted to have resulted from the abolition of abortion (see Chapter 7). Even if population pressure had been unbearably high, we would not have an explanation of why the Siraya chose abortion, rather than infanticide, abstinence, or nonprocreative sex, to limit their population, more intensive agriculture to increase their food supply, or warfare or emigration to expand their territorial base. In sum, the tradition dating from Montesquieu that sees Sirayan mandatory abortion as an institution designed to limit population growth derives from Western intellectual traditions and preconceptions, not from the ethnography and history of the Siraya.

The Problem of Age and Reproductive Span

With this background we are ready to confront a second demographic issue raised by the institution of mandatory abortion. In the long passage cited at the beginning of Chapter 1, Candidius reports that Sirayan women aborted until ages 35, 36, or 37. In a separate account written a few months earlier, Candidius reported that Sirayan women aborted until they "reached their thirtieth, thirty-third, or thirty-fifth year" (Campbell 1903:95). Candidius thus gives a range of ages (30–37) at which Sirayan women ceased aborting, but all of them are high, and beyond the usual peak childbearing years. (For an argument as to why no specific age could be given, see Chapter 4.) Could women only beginning to give birth at such late ages have produced enough children to replenish the population? What about the demographic *consequences* of mandatory abortion?

Ferrell suggests that mandatory abortion until women reached their thirties could not have "continued very long without drastic decrease of the population" (Ferrell 1969:57; 1971:220). But the Sirayan villages were large; a 1639 report estimates that there were a thousand inhabitants each in Sinkan and Bakloan and nearly three thousand each in Soulang and Mattau (Campbell 1903:179–180).[9] The large village populations reported in 1639, before Dutch pressure to abandon abortion could have had an effect, suggest that the Sirayan population was not drastically decreasing. Sirayan villages were in a state of constant warfare and might therefore have been concerned if their populations were dwindling, yet there are no reports that they were aware of or concerned about declining numbers.

For Sirayan mandatory abortion not to have had the effect of drastically reducing population requires that two conditions be satisfied. First, the women who induced multiple miscarriages early in life must not have suffered any long-term adverse consequences to their fertility; I addressed this in Chapter 1. Second, life expectancy at birth and the reproductive span of life of Sirayan women must have been considerable to accommodate the delay of childbearing to such a late age. If this second condition is to be fulfilled, we need to answer the following questions. How many children must Sirayan women on average have borne in order to maintain a stable population? Could women above age 30 bear the required number of children? What must Sirayan life expectancy have been?

The demographer Ansley Coale calculates that an average of three births per woman, equivalent to an annual birth rate of 21.3 per thousand, is sufficient to maintain at a constant size a population with a life expectancy at birth of 47 (Coale 1974:44–45). Lower life expectancies (reflecting primarily higher rates of infant mortality) require higher birth rates to maintain a stable population; four births per woman are required to sustain a population with a life expectancy of 34, and five births are needed where life expectancy is 26. Because Coale's figures presume women who survive to reproductive age begin to bear children as early as they are able, the birth rate would have to be adjusted upward for the Siraya to accommodate the delay in childbearing caused by mandatory abortion. Could women above age 30 have produced the three children necessary to reproduce a population with a life expectancy of at least 47?

Data from two documented populations indicate that women well into their thirties are still capable of bearing more than three children. These are the Hutterites and the Irish. Hutterite women are famous for their fertility and in 1921–1930 bore an average of 12.4 children. These Hutterite women were on average bearing 5.6 children after age 30 and 3.4 children after age 35, and had a life expectancy in the high sixties.[10] The Irish are famous for combining late age at marriage (29 for women in 1925) with high marital fertility. This Irish pattern of delayed childbearing closely approximates that of the Siraya. In 1911 Irish women who married between age 30 and age 34 bore an average of 3.5 children and had a life expectancy at birth of 54.[11]

Thus, the reproductive span of women's lives was great enough to have accommodated mandatory abortion to age 30 under Hutterite and Irish conditions. We must still inquire about the life expectancy of the Siraya. Other than the qualitative evidence of good nutrition and health cited above, there is little evidence regarding Sirayan life expectancy. Candidius refers to the older men as those from 40 to 60 (Campbell 1903:11) and makes no comments that he found Sirayan life-spans unusual. Some indirect evidence of long life expectancy comes from the Ami age grade systems, which commonly list grades for men as old as age 82 (Ch'en Chi-lu 1965:94–95). Anthony Reid concludes that Southeast Asians in the seventeenth century, who rarely suffered from malnutrition and famine, had a life expectancy at birth of a little over 40. He cites one population where the average age at death for women who survived childhood was 51.5. Reid's estimate is based on impressionistic evidence and compares with a 17th-century European life expectancy of 32 (A. Reid 1988:48–50). Coale's calculations require life expectancies in the high forties if three children per woman are to be enough. Because of their low population density and the abundance of venison (see figures cited above), I argue that the Siraya enjoyed a "primitive affluence" and substantial life expectancies.

Indeed, affluence and low mortality may have made it seem unnecessary to bear the burden of raising large numbers of children. The Siraya suffered neither from the high rates of infant mortality that force women into frequent childbearing nor the poverty that counsels parental investment in many children in anticipation of the economic payback they will make. The poor get children. The affluent Siraya got abortions. Sahlins (1972) argues that primitive affluence makes possible structures of underproduction, at least for males (he ignores fertility limitation); the Sirayan case suggests the link between affluence and structures of under*re*production may be just as significant for females. Affluence may have made it possible for the Siraya to practice abortion, but affluence cannot explain why the Siraya made abortion mandatory rather than optional (a problem that I address below).

In conclusion, the Hutterite and Irish cases show that a society restricting childbearing to women in their thirties could reproduce itself and maintain a stable population. Of course, the Hutterites and the Irish, benefiting from 20th-century medicine, enjoyed life expectancies greater than we can safely predict for the primitively affluent Siraya. For the Siraya mandatory abortion beyond age 35 was definitely pushing, although I argue not exceeding, the limits of demographic possibility, if population were not to decline. Clearly we are on safer demographic ground at the lower end of the range of ages Candidius gives for the termination of aborting and the beginning of childbearing.[12]

We can certainly agree that a society practicing mandatory abortion until women reached their thirties, by foreshortening the childbearing years, could not achieve rapid population growth, and was probably at best maintaining a stable population.

Cultural Materialism: The Divale and Harris Model

In their controversial article "Population, Warfare, and the Male Supremacist Complex," William Divale and Marvin Harris (1976) present a cultural materialist theory of population control that predicts that certain forms of social organization will emerge in response to population pressure. They argue that horticultural societies seeking to achieve balance between population and resources will practice both female infanticide and warfare. Selective female infanticide will reduce the number of women and limit the ability of the population to grow, while producing a surplus of young men who can be preferentially nourished and trained as warriors. These warriors, spurred on by the sexual deprivation caused by the shortage of women, will fight to expand the resource base of their village and the honors that will win them the sexual favors of the women. In this way, female infanticide (by reducing population growth) and male warfare (by expanding the resource base) enable the group to achieve an optimal, stable population (Divale and Harris 1976:526–527). Abortion under prescientific conditions, Divale and Harris believe, is not the way to achieve this goal because abortion kills adult females as well as fetuses, and does not allow the society to selectively rear males (1976:530–531). (Divale and Harris are unaware of the medical advantages of massage abortion, but a safer means of abortion would not enable the selective rearing of males their model requires.)

Without questioning the cultural materialist and functionalist assumptions it makes,[13] let us ask how the Siraya measure up to the Divale and Harris model. The Siraya did engage in warfare to defend village territories, but they did not use a shortage of women (caused by female infanticide) to motivate it. Not only did the Siraya practice abortion and not selective female infanticide, they preferred daughters to sons, for it was daughters who would marry matrilocally and care for elderly parents (Blusse and Roessingh 1984:74; Thompson 1964:174, 180, 191). Moreover, widespread fornication and adultery, frequent divorce, and early marriage (age 21 for males) suggest that sexual deprivation was not being used to motivate male headhunting and warfare.[14] The Siraya population growth rate was limited by mandatory abortions, but if population control was their goal, the Divale and Harris model suggests that Siraya mandatory abortion was an inefficient way to achieve this goal. The failure of the Siraya to conform to Divale and Harris's model linking warfare and female infanticide suggests that either (1) the Siraya were particularly backward in their population control methods, (2) the model is defective, or (3) population pressure is not the key to explaining the Siraya practice of abortion. Any or all of these may be true, and no definitive answer can be given here; but at the very least, the argument that Siraya mandatory abortion was a response to population pressing on resources receives no support from the Divale and Harris model.

There is simply no evidence, therefore, that supports the view that Sirayan mandatory abortion was an adaptation to demographic pressure. On the contrary, low population density and the abundance of venison suggest that the Siraya were a primitive affluent society, not a society facing subsistence crises caused by overpopulation. Once we have understood how Sirayan institutions of marriage and family operated, however, I will return to ask whether there is a sense in which these institutions made the Siraya disinterested in further population growth and therefore tolerant of mandatory abortion (see Chapter 6).

Notes

1. Ferrell also speculates that mandatory abortions maximized female agricultural labor inputs; see below.

2. In 1650 Dutch control over Taiwan's aboriginal population was at its height (Nakamura 1936; Shepherd 1993:38). Nakamura has published three of the censuses from the archives, those of 1647, 1650, and 1655. Although the calculations of density are based on village data aggregated by ethnolinguistic groupings, readers should not imagine that these groups acted as tribal blocks; except for occasional intervillage alliances, there was no political organization above the village level in aboriginal Taiwan.

3. Table 1 includes only eight ethnolinguistic groups of plains aborigines and does not include other ethnolinguistic groups included in the census or populations beyond Dutch control. For all Taiwan, including some mountainous areas, the 1650 Dutch census reports a total population of 68,657 in 268 villages. If we generously estimate the population in mountain areas beyond Dutch control at 40,000, the island as a whole had a total population of less than 110,000. Spread over a gross area of 36,000 square kilometers, aboriginal population density was a low 3.1 per square kilometer. This compares to a predominantly Chinese population of three million in 1905 with a gross density of 83.3 per square kilometer. Today, employing quite different technologies, medical and productive, the population of Taiwan is 20 million and density is 555.6 persons per square kilometer.

The average area per Siraya village (21 villages in all) was 175 square kilometers, while the average area per village for the remaining seven plains aborigine groups was 66 square kilometers. Shepherd (1993:38–46) concludes that the large population of Sirayan villages was a consequence, not of ecological factors or population pressure, but of the Sirayan system of matrifocal households, duolocal residence, and male age grades. Each adult male in such a system seeks to minimize the distance between two points that claim his interest: his natal kin group where he retains membership and a position of some authority, and his wife's residence. A common solution to this "matrilineal puzzle" is to marry within the natal village. The bilateral extension of the incest taboo (which eliminates many neighbors as possible mates), however, requires that a village contain a sizeable population beyond each ego's kindred if he is to find a spouse within the village. Village endogamy was also enforced by the system of male age sets, which could only be guaranteed a permanent membership if no members were lost through out-marriage. The result was a large average village population for the Siraya, who alone among the ethnic groups covered by the Dutch censuses, had matrifocal households, duolocal residence, and male age grades, and practiced village endogamy (Shepherd 1993:38–46).

4. See Conklin 1957:146; Sahlins 1972:44; and Schlegel 1979:69. These studies describe 20th-century systems where hunting supplied very little to the diet. Densities higher than 100 per square kilometer have been observed in New Guinea (Sahlins 1972:44). Aboriginal population densities much greater than Taiwan's are reported at European contact for Polynesia, where gross densities

ranged from 12 to 68 (excluding sparsely populated New Zealand) (Kirch 1984:98). These denser populations depended to a greater extent on root crop agriculture (yam and taro, and later, sweet potatoes), and in the Polynesian cases, on fishing, than did Formosan aborigines, who nevertheless also had these food sources in their inventories.

    5. Anthony Reid estimates for much of Southeast Asia in the 17th century an average gross population density of five to six persons per square kilometer. Reid argues that the key factors keeping Southeast Asian population low were fertility limitation and warfare, and not disease or poverty (1988:14–18). The Siraya data underlines the importance of fertility limitation rather than poverty. Devastating wars of the kind Reid reports for Southeast Asian kingdoms were not, however, a factor keeping population low in Taiwan, where headhunting raids claimed many fewer victims a year. Diseases, such as malaria, probably did play an important role in Taiwan. It is likely that periodic epidemics introduced into the island from the Asian mainland helped keep the population at a low level. The Siraya, located near the island's major harbor, could have escaped few of these epidemics. A 1636 report notes an outbreak of smallpox (Campbell 1903:124). The epidemic of "ague and measles" that hit the island in 1653 (Campbell 1903:290) was an important cause of a substantial drop in reported population between 1650 and 1655. The 1650 and 1655 population totals of the four Sirayan villages nearest Tainan show the impact of the epidemic: the population of Sinkan fell from 958 to 901; Bakloan from 942 to 862; Soulang from 2093 to 1485; and Mattau from 1411 to 1196 (Nakamura 1936:3, 1937:3).

    6. These exports were generated by fields and hunters all over Taiwan's western coastal plain and thus were not limited to Sirayan territory. The largest exporting years were 1634 and 1638 when exports exceeded one hundred thousand skins. Please note that harvesting the herds on this scale for the Dutch trade was the beginning of the end for plains aborigine affluence and the traditional hunting and horticultural economies (see Shepherd 1993: passim).

    7. It is well to remember that 17th-century Dutchmen were not particularly tall. Anthony Reid concludes (after reviewing contemporary travel accounts and some archaeological reports on skeletal remains) that "on average Southeast Asians of the seventeenth century were as tall as Europeans" (Reid 1988:48). The average adult male height in the seventeenth century appears to have been about 160 centimeters or five feet three inches (Reid 1988:48; Floud et al. 1990:6, 22–23). To date, I have succeeded in locating only two additional scattered bits of evidence on aboriginal stature. A 1967 anthropometric study of Taiwan aborigines found the tallest group to be the plains dwelling Ami (thereby confirming Struys' contrast of plains to mountain dwellers), with an average adult male height of 164.6 centimeters (Chai 1967:85). Hundreds of graves from the three-thousand-year-old Peinan site in southeastern Taiwan have yielded male skeletons averaging 160 centimeters and 40 years of age at death (Ch'en Shih-chi 1982:36).

    8. With respect to Ferrell's speculation that mandatory abortion had been recently adopted in response to overpopulation, we may add the following. The Dutch reports give no indication that the Siraya population was top heavy with people of advanced age, which we might expect if mandatory abortion had been adopted in the recent past and was causing a drastic reduction in births, as Ferrell postulated. Nor is there any hint that the custom of mandatory abortion had been recently adopted; on the contrary, Sirayan women told Candidius, "Our

customs have been handed down to us from generation to generation and cannot be done away with" (Campbell 1903:95).

9. The 1650 census (taken after Dutch pressure to end abortion had begun to affect the Siraya) reports the following populations: Sinkan, 958; Bakloan, 942; Soulang, 2093; Mattau, 1411 (Nakamura 1936:3). These figures confirm the general accuracy of the 1639 estimate while suggesting that it exaggerated the populations of the larger villages of Soulang and Mattau.

10. Studies of the Hutterites, the premiere "natural fertility" population, show that in 1921–1930 Hutterite women, *after* bearing an average of nine children, were still capable at ages 35 to 49 of giving birth to an average of 3.4 children (Howell 1979:155; Eaton and Mayer 1954:25). According to South Dakota data (per Eaton and Mayer 1954:33), Hutterite life expectancy circa 1940 was in the high sixties (Grove and Hetzel 1968:312). Compared to Hutterites, Sirayan women would have benefitted from avoiding the strain of a large number of early births.

11. The Irish are well known for combining late age at marriage with high marital fertility. The Irish, like the Siraya, delayed a woman's reproductive years to her thirties (unlike the Siraya, they also delayed most sexual activity). In Ireland in 1925–1926 the average age at marriage was 29 for females and 35 for males (Kennedy 1973:139–140). Yet marital fertility was high: in 1910–1912 and 1925–1927 the annual rates were 305 and 271 births per 1000 married women aged 15–44 (Kennedy 1973:176). In 1911 Irish women married at ages 30–34 and 35–39 and averaged 352 and 213 live births (per 100 married women) after 10 to 14 years of marriage (1973:178–179). Expectation of life at birth in Ireland was 54 in 1910–1912 and 58 in 1925–1927 for both males and females (Kennedy 1973:46–48). The Irish crude birth rate (21.1 per thousand, 1911–1926 [Kennedy 1973:176]) was depressed not only by late age at marriage but also by high rates of celibacy: during this period 30% of males and 24% of females aged 45–54 are reported never married (Kennedy 1973:144). Siraya birth rates were not reduced by celibacy. The Siraya and Irish (and 1980's yuppies) resemble one another because of their pattern of delayed childbearing; the cultural reasons for the similarity are of course completely divergent for the Irish (less so for affluent yuppies).

These figures suggest that the Siraya could have practiced mandatory abortion into their thirties and maintained a stable population; but it must be emphasized that this conclusion is predicated on the assumptions that the Sirayan method of abortion did not impair a woman's fertility and that the Sirayan population as a whole was healthy and enjoyed a substantial life expectancy.

12. If the reports of women's age at the lifting of the mandatory abortion requirement were only a little exaggerated, it would be that much easier to accommodate Sirayan mandatory abortion to demographics. Because he believes that the practice of mandatory abortion for any length of time would lead to a drastic decrease of population, Ferrell queries whether Candidius has not reported too high an age for the lifting of the prohibition on bearing children (Ferrell 1969:57). Candidius in two separate accounts (and twice in one of these accounts) reports ages ranging from 30 to 37 (Campbell 1903:19, 23, 95) and in addition reports instances of women who had aborted as many as eight to sixteen times. The ages reported by Candidius agree with those reported in an earlier, independent account of the Constant and Pessaert visit to the Sirayan village of Soulang in 1623. This account states that *"they* kill these children . . . until the

time that *they* are 34 or 35 years old"(Blusse and Roessingh 1984:70, emphasis added). (Unfortunately the full text [quoted below] leaves it somewhat ambiguous as to whether "they" refers to husbands or wives.) Thus we cannot lightly dismiss the ages given in any of these reports. Additional Dutch reports, introduced below, describing how Sirayan marriage changed under Dutch missionary pressure, confirm that abortion was practiced by young married women, but do not specify ages. Certainly no other Dutch report challenges the ages given by Candidius, and there were many Dutchmen who came to know the Siraya after Candidius who could have corrected an error if one was made. We may speculate that the Siraya had some unique system of calculating years that would inflate the age given at which women were no longer subject to mandatory abortion. Indeed, Candidius remarks in several locations with respect to the men that they kept track not of their exact ages, but rather of the relative status of their age grades (Campbell 1903:15, 17). The ages that Candidius gives with respect to male life cycle and age grade events, however, are in no way unusual and correspond to the ages reported for similar events among the Ami (discussed below). Candidius certainly does not hint that the ages he gives for the life cycle events of either the men or the women are in any way unusual. Unless some new documentary evidence is uncovered contradicting Candidius, analysts of Sirayan institutions must accept the ages he has reported.

13. The Divale and Harris model is based on cultural materialist and functionalist assumptions that social institutions form integrated systems operating to further adaptation of populations to environments, and that these institutions result from selective pressures acting independently of conscious calculation. My own reading of the anthropological and historical record sees too much evidence of arbitrariness and dysfunction in human society to accept these premises. Cultural materialism also shares with functionalism an inability to explain the selection between functional equivalents, for example, why one group limits population through warfare and infanticide, and other groups through abortion, celibacy, homosexuality, and reduced coital frequency.

The Yap case also serves to question the facile assumption that practices that limit population growth, such as abortion, must be intended to adjust populations to the carrying capacities of particular techno-environments. Yap women practiced abortion in the early 20th century, when Yap's population had declined to a fraction of its historic height, despite male disapproval of abortion and expressed desire for a larger population (Schneider 1968; Devereux 1976:353–354). Yap's population declined from a total of 7,808 in 1899 to 2,582 in 1946 (a density of 25 per square kilometer) (Hunt et al. 1954:22–23). No study has confirmed, however, that the frequency of abortion on Yap was as great as Schneider's account (1968) would imply (Wolff et al. 1971; Underwood 1973); indeed, to make his argument Schneider had to ignore (his own) data on age-specific fertility in Hunt et al. 1949:40, Table V). For another study questioning the adaptive value of practices limiting population growth, see E. Roth 1993.

14. Divale and Harris hypothesize in the alternative that some societies can be expected to achieve stable population through the birth-spacing effects of prolonged lactation instead of through female infanticide and warfare, although they seem confused as to whether protein surpluses or deficits will encourage delayed weaning (1976:531, 533). As the Siraya did engage in warfare, they also fail to conform to this alternative.

4

Institutional Analysis

Sirayan Marriage and Family

As population pressure cannot explain Sirayan mandatory abortion, we must make sense of Sirayan practices by reconstructing the cultural context and meaning of Sirayan marriage, family, and definitions of gender.[1] Let us begin by describing Sirayan courtship and marriage.

Sirayan boys were required to wear short hair until they reached age 17 and began to shave; then they were allowed to grow their hair past their ears. When their hair had grown long they began "to woo" and to have lovers, but, Candidius tells us, they were not allowed to marry until they reached age 20 or 21 (Campbell 1903:17–18, 24). Girls married as early as they were thought physically fit to do so, presumably at puberty (Campbell 1903:18; Coyett 1975:7).

A Sirayan youth contracted a marriage by sending a female relative to the house where the girl who had caught his fancy resided. There his representative made the proposal and displayed marriage gifts intended for the bride. Approval of the proposal by the girl's parents was signaled by acceptance of the gifts; this concluded the marriage without further ceremony. The young man was allowed to pass the *following* night with his bride.[2]

The payment of the marriage gifts (which Candidius calls "dowry") entitled the Sirayan husband to exclusive sexual access to his bride but did not give him control over her labor or the right to remove her or her children from her natal home. The value of the marriage gifts reflected the wealth of the groom's family, but Candidius does not report that the rights of the husband over his wife varied according to the amounts paid. The gifts were personal items and consisted of armlets and bracelets made of bamboo, finger rings of metal and antler, deerskin leggings, and a variety of garments and textiles, some made of dog's hair and some acquired in trade from the Chinese.[3]

Once the marriage was contracted, the husband was allowed to visit his wife in her home only on very strict terms; he had to "steal in like a thief" at night and leave "like a cat sneaking out of a hencoop" before daybreak. These are the visits "by stealth" that caught the attention of Malthus. During these nocturnal conjugal visits, the husband was not

allowed to speak to or approach members of the wife's household. Nor
could the husband enter his wife's house during the day unless all the
other women of the household were absent and he obtained his wife's
permission, which she was entitled to withhold (see also Blusse and
Roessingh 1984:69, 74).

Sirayan marriage was ideally monogamous. Candidius states that
there were some men who had two wives but that such cases were rare
and "not considered a proper or right thing," (Campbell 1903:20).

Among the Siraya, divorce was easily obtained and nearly as common as adultery. The husband could leave his wife and marry another,
but if no reason other than pleasure were offered, he could not reclaim
the marriage gifts. If the wife had "committed adultery, or followed
other men, or has struck her husband, or committed any other misde-
meanour", however, the husband could demand repayment of the
marriage gifts. Candidius seems to imply that the woman could for
similar reasons divorce her husband. In cases of adultery where divorce
was not desired, the husband could claim as compensation two or three
pigs from the stable of his wife's paramour, but no such remedy is
mentioned as available to a wronged wife (Campbell 1903:17).[4]

These rights to payment in cases of adultery, and divorce occa-
sioned by adultery, confirm that Sirayan marriage was expected to
create a relationship of exclusive sexual access between spouses, although there is some suggestion of a double standard.[5] But as Candidius
notes, the Siraya did not "regard fornication and adultery as sins, if
committed in secret," (Campbell 1903:23–24); "the men are great whore-
mongers: for, although they have their own wives, they neglect no
opportunity of committing adultery. It is, however, a rule that the wife
of the husband and the husband of the wife should remain in ignorance
of it," (Campbell 1903:20). To Candidius the frequency of adultery
explained the frequency of divorce; the passages discussed below suggest that both phenomena were the consequence of institutions creating
a weak marital bond.

After marriage Sirayan women remained with their natal families.
The men, before and after marriage, divided their time between their
natal families, where their mothers and sisters cooked for them, and
men's houses, where they conducted most of their business and slept:

> [T]he rule is for unmarried men, and men who, though married, do not sleep
> with their wives, to have separate places in the village appointed them
> where they pass the night. Every group of twelve or fourteen houses has its
> own separate dormitory; and these dormitories being supplied with sleep-
> ing-berths, which are occupied at night by the men, and even by children
> [boys] . . . [down to] four years of age; each one sleeping in the dormitory
> to which he belongs. [Campbell 1903:21]

Boys and men were probably assigned to these dormitories on the basis of some combination of ward membership and age grade duty, as it is likely that dormitories were positioned at each entrance to the village and served as guard houses.[6] It appears that married men had plenty of occasion to sleep in the men's house, as the third of the 27 commandments setting forth the taboos to be observed for ten days every month states, "No Married-men shall sleep with their Wives in the time of *Karichang*" (Shepherd 1986:72, 75).[7]

Economic cooperation between young husbands and wives was practically nonexistent. Candidius reports:

> The women possess their own fields with the women-folk of their own generation. These they cultivate for their own support. They always live together, and eat and drink in the same house. The husband follows the same rule; he and his folk possessing their own fields, and he remaining in his own house with his own kindred. The wife does not garner for the husband, nor the husband for the wife: each house provides for itself. [Campbell 1903:19]

On the basis of these passages, anthropologists will readily associate Sirayan marriage with the Nayar, Ashanti, Minangkabau, and Moso examples of that rare category, a matrilineal system practicing duolocal (natolocal) residence, in which husband and wife even after marriage do not set up joint housekeeping but continue to live apart, each in his or her respective natal home (Gough 1961; Schneider 1961; Fox 1967:100–103; Fortes 1970; Shih C. 1993). The Siraya, however, insisted on separate, duolocal residence of husband and wife only during the first twenty or so years of marriage. And even after this long period the Siraya still did not give the husband the right to remove his wife from her natal family; instead it was the husband who then left his natal family to take up uxorilocal residence with his wife:

> When the husbands reach the age of fifty, they leave their hereditary property, their dwellings, and their kith and kin to take up their permanent abode with their wives, who, of course, are now stricken in years. But they are seldom at home; the greater part of their time being spent in the fields, where they build a hut to sleep in at night. [Campbell 1903:20, as corrected by Blusse and Roessingh 1984:78]

Elsewhere Candidius tells us that Sirayan practice was for married couples to take up joint residence after the husband reached age 40:

> The older men—those from forty to sixty—are generally in the fields with their wives day and night. There, small huts are built, in which they rest and sleep, and for about two months at a time they do not appear in the village unless some festivity or other is going on. [Campbell 1903:11][8]

In the passages cited above, Candidius states that joint uxorilocal residence began when the men reached either 40 or 50. The transition in residence most probably took place when a man reached his early forties, for it was at this point that another important transition in the life of Sirayan men took place. Candidius informs us that when men reached age 40 they served for two years as village councillors (the highest political rank), after which they retired from office and another age grade succeeded them (Campbell 1903:15). Putting these passages together provides the key to understanding Siraya marriage. Men married at age 21; women married at puberty. Thus when men reached senior status after age 40 and took up uxorilocal residence, their wives were in their thirties, which is the age at which mandatory abortion was no longer required.[9]

Candidius' reports that women aborted until they were "thirty-five, thirty-six, or thirty-seven," or until their "thirtieth, thirty-third, or thirty-fifth year" (Campbell 1903:19, 95) and the Constant and Pessaert report that parents killed children until "they are 34 or 35 years old" (Blusse and Roessingh 1984:70) are misleading because they take the age of the woman as the key to terminating the period of mandatory abortion. The reason these reports cannot specify a definite age after which a woman was allowed to bear children is because it was the age of the husband and not the age of his younger wife which was crucial. I argue that only after the husband had served a full term in the ranks of the age grade system was he allowed to take up joint residence with his wife and to father children.

Thus on my interpretation, the Siraya adhered to an ideal of marriage that led to the creation of a uxorilocally resident conjugal family; but the demands of the male age grade system in conjunction with the institution of mandatory abortion for young wives prevented the creation of these families until the husband had completed his age grade service.[10] Thus Siraya married couples lived jointly and bore children only at a relatively late age.[11]

Male Age Grades

Seen from this perspective Sirayan marriage and abortion cannot be understood without regard to the male age grade system and the Sirayan construction of male gender. In his discussion of Sirayan notions of prestige, Candidius emphasized the importance of age over all other status rankings:

> They consider age to be the great mark of distinction; and show more respect
> for it than on account of any one's mere social position, power, or riches.
> Thus, when two persons meet on the road or in the street, the younger will
> invariably go a little out of the way for the elder, and turn his back towards
> him till he has passed; and even when younger persons meet on the road
> and speak on matters of business, they will take great care to turn their backs
> to an older person till he has entirely passed by. When an older man bids a
> younger one do anything for him, the latter will not have the courage to
> refuse to do it, although he should require to go two, three, or four miles to
> execute the commission. In company the younger will never venture to
> speak while the older ones are doing so. At their public meals, or when they
> meet to drink, they invariably serve the more aged persons first; age alone
> being considered. They show their respect for each other in this way.
> [Campbell 1903:17]

Senior men thus were able to command obedience from other adult but
junior men on the basis of their age grade rank alone. The avoidance
behaviors by which juniors showed respect for seniors suggests that the
system was highly regimented and enforced with some discipline.

Now let us consider the life cycle of the Sirayan male as he passed
through the age grade system. Sirayan boys stayed with their mothers
until they were four, when they began to sleep in the men's dormitories
(Campbell 1903:19, 21). Until they reached age 15 to 17 they were
forbidden to "let their hair grow longer than just to cover their ears"
(Campbell 1903:17). At about 17 they were allowed to grow their hair
"as long as they like"; the fashion was for adult men to wear their hair
long, "hanging without braids" (Campbell 1903:18; Blusse and Roessingh 1984:74). Seventeen appears to be the age at which young men
entered the age-set ranks. (There is no description of any age set intitia-
tion for Siraya as is recorded for the Ami.) Also at 17 the boys began to
court and find lovers (Campbell 1903:18, 24).

Marriage came at age twenty-one for the boys:

> The men must have attained to the age of twenty or twenty-one before they
> can marry; for, although this people do not keep any account of years, they
> thoroughly remember who is older and who is younger. Those who are born
> in the same month, or in the same half or whole year, are considered to have
> been born at the same time, and to be of the same age. In their language this
> is called *saat cassiuwang*. On reaching this age they may marry; but those
> who are *cassiuwang*, or too young, may not marry. This they remember and
> never fail to observe. [Campbell 1903:17][12]

The sexual division of labor was especially sharp among young adults.
Young women did all the domestic chores and housekeeping (Blusse
and Roessingh 1984:70, 73) as well as the agricultural labor.[13] According
to Candidius:

> The women, who are complete drudges, do most of the farming work. . . .
> While the women work, the men go about doing nothing, especially the
> strong young men from seventeen to twenty-four years of age. . . . the
> younger men seldom assist their wives in the fields; their principal occupa-
> tions being hunting and fighting. [Campbell 1903:10–11]

The men hunted deer in groups, sometimes with dogs. Deer teemed all
over Taiwan in those days, and as we have seen, the Siraya ate much
venison. They also traded large quantities of deerskins and dried meat
(for salt and textiles) through Chinese village traders to China and Japan
(Campbell 1903:11–12; Blusse and Roessingh 1984:69–70; Coyett 1975:2).

Intervillage warfare was endemic to the Siraya and was linked to
headhunting. The men devoted considerable energy to military training
and carrying out raids on neighboring villages. The greatest glory and
the highest prestige was bestowed on successful headhunters. The report of the Constant and Pessaert trip gives a graphic description of the
men's war exercises:

> The men are daily trained on the public markets, which are quite large and
> five in number. They exercise with—and race against—each other, sparring
> with bamboos or reeds, each seeking to gain advantage over the other . . .
> One man beats a drum, of a braced deerhide . . . just as there are drums and
> trumpets in our exercises.
> The aforesaid young men, although stark naked, decorate their head,
> waist and arms with green stuff more or less like Bacchus is depicted,
> mantled in ivy. Others wear garlands around their head, arms and waist,
> which are plaited from the flat part of the deer's tail and painted in all kinds
> of colours. They seem to take great pride in them. [Blusse and Roessingh
> 1984:75]

These exercises imbued the young men with a martial spirit and a
warrior ideal. Warriors used shields, swords, and spears in combat.
Sirayan warfare consisted primarily of sending out and warding off
raiding parties of headhunters:

> In their wars, they have no captains or chiefs, but any one who has got
> possession of many heads, or who is considered to have cut off a head, in
> short, any one who feels inclined for fighting, can easily get ten or twenty
> men to regard him as their nominal chief and to follow him in waging war
> or in pretending to do so. [Campbell 1903:13]

The importance of natural leadership in warfare is brought out in the
report of the Constant and Pessaert expedition:

> We have not found any signs of the existence of chieftains among them . . .
> The bravery by which they come into esteem consists in bringing home as
> many of the enemy's heads as possible from the war (and the men do

nothing else than waging war). Those are considered the most excellent among them. [Blusse and Roessingh 1984:70, see also 75]

Warriors who returned with enemy heads were welcomed as heroes; such events were occasions for several days of feasting and celebration (Campbell 1903:14–15).

These heroes received some preferential treatment in the distribution of game taken in hunting expeditions (Blusse and Roessingh 1984:75), but could not achieve political power within their villages until their age set reached forty and they were chosen to succeed to the rank of councillor. Each village had a standing committee of "men of good repute." These councillors, though lacking the power to issue commands or make laws, took the lead in deliberative assemblies which they convened to consider proposals and decide disputes and in which they displayed their oratorical skills (Campbell 1903:15).[14]

Such an assembly is described in the report of the Constant and Pessaert expedition:

> [Councillors] receive a seat, or, as we say, a cushion (to sit on) among those who are in government or in office, when they daily appear before sunrise on one of the markets (upon the beating of the drumskin). There all men, young and old, gather in number. They discuss the cases that occur, and the humblest person possesses as much vote as the most exalted one. [Blusse and Roessingh 1984:75]

Candidius tells us that men reached the rank of councillor when their age set cohort came of age:

> Every two years the councillors lay down their office, and others are chosen in their stead. Councillors must be about forty years of age, and all of them of the same age. Although they know nothing of the number of years, and no one really knows how long he has lived, still they do remember on what day, and in what year and month, they were born. When councillors have been in office two years, each causes the hair on both sides of his forehead to be plucked out, which is a sign that he has fulfilled his term and is no longer in office. Then, other councillors of the same age are chosen. [Campbell 1903:15][15]

Thus the headhair that had been allowed to grow long upon entry into adulthood at age 17 was partially removed after age 40, upon retirement from age grade service and the transition to uxorilocal residence.[16]

Thus conjugal family life began so late for Sirayan men and women because of the demands of the male age grade system and the culture of warfare. These required men until their forties to devote exclusive attention to the affairs of intervillage headhunting and the winning of prestige in warfare. Mandatory abortions by young wives and postpon-

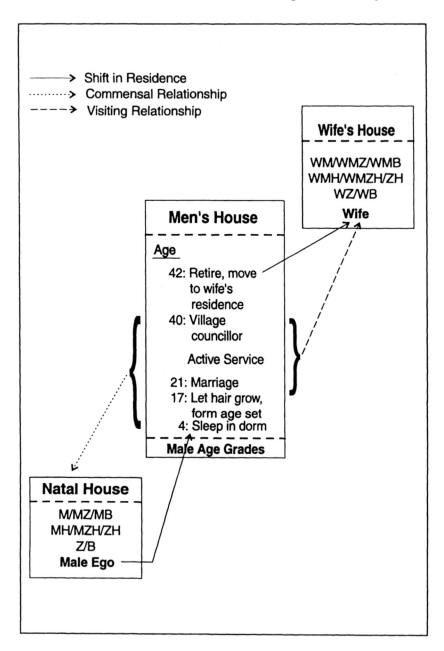

Figure 2
Schematic Representation of Sirayan Social Structure (Male Point of View).
W = wife('s), M = mother('s), Z = sister('s), B = brother, and H = husband.

ing conjugal family life were deemed a necessary complement to this pattern of male age grade service. (See Figure 2.)

We may note here some characteristics of the Sirayan conjugal household once it was established. The delayed transfer of the husband's residence to his wife's household minimized the tension we might expect to find in matrifocal households between a son-in-law and his father-in-law in competing for the services of the wife/daughter. During the first twenty years of marriage, duolocal residence separated the wife's father and her husband, and the wife's economic services belonged entirely to her natal household. When the husband finally did take up uxorilocal residence, his parents-in-law, if they had survived to that time, were at an advanced and increasingly dependent age;[17] thus they were unlikely to be in a position to challenge the authority of the uxorilocally resident husband. In this way delayed transfer assured the adult male upon his retirement from active age grade service that he was moving not into a subordinate position in his wife's family, but into a position of responsibility and authority. It is even possible that the inconsistency in the ages Candidius gives for the timing of the move to joint residence (40 or 50) reflects a preference on the part of some males to await the demise of the wife's father before taking up uxorilocal residence. Nor would the husband's authority be seriously challenged by his wife's brothers, for the husband would be senior in age grade status to any of his wife's brothers who had not yet themselves taken up uxorilocal residence elsewhere. It appears likely that men retained close ties to their natal kin, and may have returned to their natal households when ill or dying, and to the men's house if they divorced or the wife died.[18]

Delayed Transfer Uxorilocal Marriage

Sirayan marriage appears, therefore, to have been a two-stage process, the first stage being that of male age grade service, separate residence, and abortion, followed by a second stage of the husband's retirement from age grade service, joint uxorilocal residence, and the bearing of children. This form of marriage we may term duo-uxorilocal, or delayed transfer uxorilocal marriage, referring to the delay in the husband's taking up residence with his wife.[19]

Two additional pieces of evidence support this reconstruction of Sirayan marriage. These involve reading two of the classic passages that report mandatory abortion together with the text that immediately surrounds them. The paragraph in Candidius's Account that describes mandatory abortion sits between two others. The first paragraph tells us that Siraya married couples did not cooperate economically and that Siraya husbands needed their wives' permission to visit during the day. The next paragraph begins explaining that children remained with their mothers in their early years, goes on to describe the custom of mandatory abortion, and concludes by telling us that only women who have reached 37 to 38 years give live birth. The immediately succeeding paragraph then informs us that when husbands reach fifty they take up residence with their wives (Campbell 1903:19–20). Although Candidius never directly links the shift in postmarital residence (from separate [duolocal] to uxorilocal) to the lifting of the mandatory abortion requirement and the bearing of children, his order of presentation can be read to imply such an argument: young couples live separately (paragraph 1); women abort until their thirties and then give live birth (paragraph 2); men at 50 coreside with their wives (paragraph 3). Indeed, Malthus read these paragraphs in just this fashion, although he mistakenly assumed (applying European models of the patriarchal family) that the wife left her father's residence for that of her husband (Malthus 1989:56).

The second piece of evidence, which comes from the report of the 1623 expedition of Constant and Pessaert, directly links the end of a husband's headhunting career to the termination of the practice of infanticide:

> The bravery by which they come into esteem consists in bringing home as many of the enemy's heads as possible from the war (and the men do nothing else than waging war). Those are considered the most excellent among them . . . As long as the men go to war and generate children with their wives, *they kill these children up to the time that they do not go to war any more*. This is the case (as we have seen from some and others) until the time that they are 34 or 35 years old. [Blusse and Roessingh 1984:70, emphasis added][20]

Constant and Pessaert's informant made the link for them: no children were reared so long as *husbands* served as warriors. Only when husbands retired from age grade service and headhunting after 40 did their wives begin to bear the children they conceived. We need only add Candidius's observation that men after 40 took up residence with their wives to complete our reconstruction of the Sirayan system of delayed transfer uxorilocal marriage.

The many similarities that scholars have noted between the Siraya and the matrilineal Ami and Puyuma of Taiwan's east coast (see Figure 1) enable us to make controlled comparisons that lend further support to this reconstruction of Siraya marriage (cf. Eggan 1954). The marriage systems of the Ami and the Puyuma reflect the same tensions between uxorilocal conjugal families and male age grade service which we have identified in the Sirayan system.

Ami boys in the Nan-shih area began at age 15 to live in the men's dormitories. There they received preparatory physical training and instruction in adult male skills and Ami traditions. At about age 20 young men were grouped into age sets and initiated into the *kapax*, or service rendering, grade in which they remained until age 40. The *kapax* grade was divided into three subgrades, the first of which lasted until age 26 and was the stage of the most severe training and most active service. Only after completion of the first subgrade were men allowed to marry, which they did uxorilocally. Training in the next two *kapax* subgrades was less severe and, unless they were on duty, the men were allowed to stay with their conjugal families rather than in the dormitories. Around age 41 men graduated into the superintending grade of elders (*matoasai* or *karas*) and were exempted from service and duties in the dormitories (Ch'en Chi-lu 1965:94–96).[21] Thus the Nan-shih Ami resolved the conflict their institutions created between uxorilocal conjugal families and age grade service by delaying (uxorilocal) marriage until after the men had completed the most arduous years of service at age 26. The Siraya, by contrast, allowed men to marry at age 21 but mandated abortions and forbade conjugal coresidence until men graduated from age grade service in their forties. Thus, although the Siraya allowed earlier marriage, the demands of the Siraya age grade organization seem much more extreme.

The Puyuma resolved the conflict in a different way. Boys entered the Puyuma age grade system at 14 for five years of preparatory training. Upon reaching 19 young men passed through a headhunting initiation and then entered a three-year stage of arduous training. During this period they lived in the men's house, were subject to strict obedience to their seniors, and were forbidden intercourse with females. Upon completion of this stage at age 22, men were allowed to marry uxorilocally (Ch'en Chi-lu 1965:100–103). The Puyuma thus allowed men to marry and to take up uxorilocal residence at a relatively young age, but only after enforcing sexual abstinence during their most arduous years of service. (It remains unclear in the Puyuma case whether young married men continued to have duties that required them to stay in the dormitories or men's houses.) In contrast to the Siraya, the Puyuma denied premarital sex to boys aged 19 to 21, but allowed them to marry and coreside with their wives at age 22.

Sirayan mandatory abortion and delayed transfer uxorilocal marriage can thus be seen as an extreme solution to a tension common to societies where male age grades competed with matrifocal households for the energies of young adult males. The Sirayan solution fits at one end of a spectrum of possible solutions to the problem of accommodating the creation of conjugal families to male age grade service. Compared to the Ami and Puyuma, the Siraya subjected young males to age grade discipline for a much longer period of their lives and as a consequence mandated abortion for young wives.

To sum up the argument so far, I see Sirayan mandatory abortion as a concomitant of the Sirayan system of delayed transfer uxorilocal marriage and male age grade service. Advocates of the population pressure argument, on the other hand, assume that the meaning of a practice like mandatory abortion is transparent; that its consequence (reducing population growth) is the same as its meaning (rather than a by-product thereof), and therefore must be intended (consciously, or by some invisible hand like natural selection) to limit population. The demographic approach assumes that investigating the cultural meaning and institutional context of abortion and why the Siraya use abortion and not some other form of population control (infanticide, celibacy, nonprocreative sex) is of secondary importance. Such assumptions are unwarranted in the case of Sirayan mandatory abortion, where no evidence of overpopulation or looming subsistence crisis exists. The argument here is that mandatory abortion must be understood as a Sirayan solution to a problem their social organization creates: that of accommodating male age grade service to conjugal family life. This social structural argument sees the role of abortion as enabling not population limitation, but the delay of conjugal family formation.

But note that I have not yet explained why the Siraya used abortion rather than some other means of fertility limitation or childrearing to delay the formation of families and satisfy the demands of the age grade regimen. Infanticide, fostering, adoption, celibacy, and nonprocreative sex can all be used to delay family formation; in that sense they are all "functional equivalents" of abortion, and could equally well have been used to accommodate exclusive male age grade service.[22] To explain the cultural preference for mandatory abortion requires that we investigate Sirayan religious concepts. The extreme demands of Sirayan male age grade service remain a key to helping explain why the beliefs discussed below took such an exaggerated form.

Notes

1. The following description is based on Candidius's Account in Campbell (1903:18–21), except where otherwise noted.

2. The reference to the "following" night is repeated twice (Campbell 1903:18, 19) and appears intentional. When Ami youths married (uxorilocally), they returned to the men's dormitory to spend the first night with their age

mates, and only slept with their brides on the succeeding night (Ch'en Wen-te 1986:55). Other preparations delayed the union of the Siraya couple. Before the girl entered into sexual relations with her new husband, "two of the upper teeth are knocked out of her mouth with stones, so that one can see whether she is married or not" (Blusse and Roessingh 1984:74). That removal of a girl's teeth was associated with marriage is confirmed indirectly by Wright who reports that during the monthly period of taboo or *karichang*, activities which constituted the contraction of a marriage were forbidden; thus commandments 3, 20, and 21 forbid espousal, payment of marriage gifts, consummation of a marriage, a bridegroom walking with his bride, and parents knocking out a daughter's two upper teeth (Shepherd 1986:75–76). As we know other Taiwan aboriginal cultures associate these teeth with nonhuman animality (Ch'en Chi-lu 1968:254–255), their removal appears to have symbolized the socialization of the bride's sexual powers and reproductive capacity (cf. T. Turner 1980:119–120). Miyauchi (1940:31) reports that the Tevorang Siraya were still extracting teeth as late as the late 19th century.

3. These exchanges differ from the practice reported for some Ami villages where uxorilocal postmarital residence meant that brides were required to perform groomservice to compensate their husband's natal families for the loss of a son (Bischofberger 1972; cf. also Nash 1968 and Billig 1992).

4. In fact, it is possible that such pigs were not the adulterous man's private property but the property of his natal household and female kinsmen, as it was women who tended domestic pigs.

5. Sirayan husbands appear to have acquired the right to confer sexual access to their wives on important male guests, or at least tolerated adultery in such an instance. The Dutch visitors in 1623 report:

> They do not seem to be very jealous about their wives, nor do they deem the act of procreation improper; because it happened to us, being there, that a man having used his wench (spoken with reverence) in a natural way (and that in our presence), took her by the hand and led her to us, to do the same with her and replace him in his labour; this we refused, to their astonishment (being an un-Christian act). [Blusse and Roessingh 1984:74]

This practice is confirmed in a later Chinese report by Yü Yung-ho: "A husband, seeing a guest becoming intimate with his wife, is very pleased" (Thompson 1964:192–193). Examples of host wife-sharing are widely reported in the ethnographic literature (and cannot be dismissed as boasting by guests) (Westermarck 1922:228–239).

6. The Ami distinguished dormitories, which guarded the entrances to the village, from the men's house, which was associated with a public square, skull rack, and altar (Ch'en Chi-lu 1965:93). Soulang may have had seven wards, for it is reported to have had seven "churches" and a council of seven principals (Blusse and Roessingh 1984:71, 75). Two of these wards, however, apparently joined with other wards in age grade activities, for there were only five public markets "with pavilions and other public houses," (Blusse and Roessingh 1984:75, 76). Soulang's wards were much larger than Sinkan's (if the districts described for these two villages are indeed comparable), for Sinkan is reported to have 14 "parishes" for a population (1047) less than half that of Soulang (2600) (Campbell 1903:96, 179). Candidius tells us that in Sinkan there was an idol house for every 15 to 16 families and a dormitory for every 12 to 14 houses (Campbell 1903:15, 21, 76), but there is no suggestion that Sinkan's age grade organization

was not united for the whole village. In 1650, Sinkan is reported to have had a population of 958 spread among 124 households; 124 households divided among 14 parishes would yield 9 households per parish, smaller than the idol house and dormitory groups of 12 to 16 households described by Candidius. In 1650 Soulang is reported to have had a population of 2093 spread among 241 households; seven wards would average 34 households each.

Blusse and Roessingh have suggested that Siraya wards may have corresponded to exogamous matriclans (1984:68), but I think this unlikely on a variety of grounds. First, neither Candidius nor Constant and Pessaert seem to have been impressed by the existence of corporate descent groups. Second, I suspect that the presence of a strong male age grade system reduced the role of matriclans and matrilineages in organizing political relations among males and households. Comparison with the Ami of Vataan supports this view. First, Ami matriclans were not corporate kin groups and were not exogamous (Liu Pin-hsiung 1965:62, 261). Second, the local organization of Vataan was complex and was based on wards and age grades, not matriclans. Vataan, with a population of 2362 in 1960, was composed of seven matriclans spread among six wards. Half the population of the village was categorized as belonging to one matriclan; the members of this matriclan predominated in the three older wards. The six other matriclans were spread among the remaining three "immigrant" wards. So there was no simple correspondence between matriclan and ward memberships. Although Vataan had a unified age grade organization in living memory, villagers claimed that three of the wards were immigrant wards and had each had separate age grade organizations in the past (Liu Pin-hsiung 1965:48, 62, 170, 259). Bontoc (Northern Luzon) wards have been similarly confused for lineages by ethnographers working in the descent group paradigm; see L. Reid 1972.

7. It is possible that some Siraya women avoided pregnancy and, therefore, abortions as a result of this ten-day taboo period, but it is highly unlikely that this taboo period afforded a reliable method of avoiding pregnancies.

8. Living in huts in the fields during the agricultural season would be reasonably safe because the Siraya ritual calendar, like that of other Taiwan groups, separated the agricultural season from the headhunting season (see Shepherd 1986:28 and Ho T'ing-jui 1956b:198 overleaf).

9. That the age discrepancy between husband and wife was preserved despite divorces and remarriages should not be surprising; empirical evidence of this phenomenon for an Ami village is given in Okada Yuzuru (1942:281). It seems probable that the frequency of divorce declined as couples aged.

10. Readers may ask why young Siraya bothered to marry, given the few advantages marriage seems to confer, but clearly the Siraya held to an ideal of marriage despite divided residence, adultery, and divorce. In this respect the Siraya differ little from modern Americans.

11. Candidius leaves us with one unclear reference regarding the social units that bore the burden of rearing children:

> If children are born to them, they mostly remain with their mother in her house; but when they reach the age of two, three or older, they also frequently live with *the fathers*. [Campbell 1903:19, as corrected by Blusse and Roessingh 1984:78, emphasis added]

This passage should be read to mean that young children (surely boys and not girls are meant) went to live in the men's dormitories, interpreting "fathers" to mean male authority figures rather than genitors. In a matrilineal society male authority over children would be exercised by the mother's brothers, as well as (uxorilocally) resident fathers, and in the age grade system perhaps all senior males had authority over boys. (Relying in part on Campbell's—and Grothe's 1886—corrupted version of this passage, Wang Sung-hsing [1964] attributed avunculocal residence to the Siraya, in his attempt to reconstruct the Siraya kinship system.) If "fathers" is read narrowly to mean genitors, then this passage contradicts other passages indicating that senior men who father children take up residence uxorilocally, including the reference to the role of the father and the parents in accepting proposals of marriage for their daughters. When the passage is read in the way I have proposed, it agrees with the following passage cited earlier:

> Every group of twelve or fourteen houses has its own separate dormitory; and these dormitories being supplied with sleeping-berths, which are occupied at night by the men, and even by children [boys] . . . [down to] four years of age; each one sleeping in the dormitory to which he belongs. [Campbell 1903:21]

Young girls were kept at home with their mothers (and uxorilocally resident fathers), so that by age four there was already a sharp distinction in the way boys and girls were reared. The report of the Constant and Pessaert expedition gives the following impressions:

> They bring up their children in a hard and careless way; yet they love the girls more than the boys, which they seem to show by giving more ornaments to wear to the girls, as bracelets, coral and other baubels, they being for the rest just as naked; the girls are carried on arm and shoulder more often than the boys, who run around without being looked after. [Blusse and Roessingh 1984:74]

Girls thus were encouraged to be devoted and attached to their parents, and boys to be independent and self-reliant, in anticipation of their adult roles. When the missionaries attempted to require boys to attend school, however, they discovered that parents also expected boys to help in the fields (Campbell 1903:149).

12. Sander Adelaar, who is currently working on the linguistic reconstruction of the Siraya language (1994), suggests that *saat cassiuwang* may be translated as "of the same name group" (personal communication, 1995). Candidius's use of this term seems to point to the adoption of a group name for an age set at its formation. Candidius gives age ranges for these events probably because boys close in age were grouped together in age sets. Among the Ami such cohorts were initiated in ceremonies that were held only every few years; the boys initiated together remained members of the same age set for the rest of their lives. With the passage of time, age sets graduated through a series of hierarchical age grades ranked by seniority and assigned specific duties and privileges. Several age sets, ranked by age, might occupy the same rung in the hierarchy of age grades, but strict seniority among age sets would never be violated (Ch'en Chi-lu 1965:93–96; cf. Bernardi 1985:17). In Taiwan, village political structures based on regimental age grade systems occur among the matrilineal Ami and the Puyuma. Ami villages varied in using cyclical and lineal age set naming systems. The Nan-shih Ami used a fixed nine-name sequence that repeated cyclically. The Ma-lan Ami gave each age set a unique name that passed out of use when the last member died. Individual villages recognized different num-

bers of age grades, with preparatory, severe training, service rendering, super-intending, and retired stages commonly distinguished (Ch'en Chi-lu 1965:93–95; cf. Bernardi 1985:36). The Puyuma also had a strict age grade hierarchy but appear to have put less emphasis on the unity of age sets, so that boys moved individually through the grades according to their own age (Ch'en Chi-lu 1965:100–101). Matrilineal kinship and uxorilocal marriage divided the loyalties of men between their natal households and their conjugal families; male political authority thus could not be structured on the basis of kinship groups in the way that is possible in patrilineal and virilocal systems, and instead was organized by the age grade system (see Appendix B).

13. Ferrell has speculated that female horticultural labor may be the key to explaining Sirayan marriage and abortion. Ferrell argues that mandatory abor-tion until a woman reached her thirties ensured that a woman's own lineage benefitted exclusively from her prime years of agricultural productivity (Ferrell 1969:57, 1971:220). Mandatory abortions hardly seem necessary to obtain this result, as women married uxorilocally and a woman's children became members of her household and "lineage" and not her husband's. But there can be little doubt that childbearing interfered with and made more burdensome female agricultural tasks, although, except perhaps for nursing, women in extended matrifocal households could easily have shared childcare. Considerations re-garding female labor might recommend the use of abortion to space children but are inadequate to explain an institution that radically postpones childbear-ing. Furthermore, as the Dutch desired to increase local agricultural production (to feed their garrisons), it is significant that no Dutchman ever questioned whether the missionary effort to abolish abortion and encourage conjugal coresi-dence might have the effect of reducing agricultural output. The Dutch in general considered the Siraya to be lazy and indifferent farmers, a picture inconsistent with a society anxiously trying to maximize female labor input conjured up by the argument that mandatory abortion somehow benefitted agriculture. While we do not know how hide processing was organized, I would like to point out that similar objections would apply to any argument that mandatory abortions maximized the female labor available for hide processing. (I have as yet no information on who cleaned and tanned the hides and dried the meat.) Such an argument is also contradicted by the fact that the Dutch were seeking to both abolish abortion and maximize deerskin exports and never expressed any objection that the two goals were in conflict.

The Iban offer a modern parallel to the Sirayan sexual division of labor. Among the Iban, young married men also avoided all agricultural labor other than clearing of swiddens and spent much of their time abroad on "journeys" and in headhunting. Not until age 35 and after did men settle down to manage farms and cooperate with their wives in agriculture. Iban women did not, however, postpone childbearing to their thirties (Freeman 1970:222–228). For additional examples of leisured young men and hardworking elders, see Sahlins 1972:52–55.

14. If the Nan-shih Ami may be taken as an example, it is likely that the Sirayan council system was much more complex than Candidius's description indicates. Among the Nan-shih Ami each age set had two leaders, a monitor and a chief warrior. There were villagewide councils of at least four kinds (monitors, chief warriors, elders, and all adult men), each with its own functionally distinct jurisdiction (Ch'en Chi-lu 1965:96–97).

15. Candidius, in a passage cited earlier, refined his account to suggest that rather than remembering exact calendric age, members of age sets considered themselves to be of the same age and knew precisely who was older and who younger (Campbell 1903:17).

16. Candidius reports that the Siraya removed unwanted hair by plucking and that "[t]hey have a great dislike to beards for which reason they in the same way remove the hair on the face as well as on other parts of the body" (Campbell 1903:18; see also Struys in Campbell 1903:255). These customs match those of the Ami, who also removed hair from arm pits and private parts, and indicated rank in the active *kapax* grade by plucking eyebrows (Ch'en Chi-lu 1968:257–258; Miyauchi 1940:29–30; on the Puyuma, see Ch'en Chi-lu 1965:102). Depilation of beard, temples, and genitals is also reported among Austronesian groups in the Philippines (Jenks 1905:41–42; Cole 1922:439; Garvan 1929:56; Scott 1975:28, 110, 134, 143).

17. When men in their forties took up uxorilocal residence and began to father children by wives at least 30 years old, the wives' fathers must have been at least 70 (40+30), and the wives' mothers must have been at least 60 (30+30).

18. Adult Ami men when suffering from serious illness or near death return to their natal households to be nursed by their mothers and sisters, even after years of coresidence with their wives (personal communication, Huang Hsuan-wei, 1990). This indicates that men retained membership in their natal households and that marriage did not affect these residual rights.

19. Two reports indicate that not all Sirayan villages practiced delayed transfer marriage or abortion. Although Candidius states explicitly that his Account applies to Sinkan, Mattau, Soulang, Bakloan and Tefurang (Tevorang, Ta-wu-lung) (Campbell 1903:9), when Tevorang was visited in 1636, Governor Putmans reported:

> The married men live in the same houses with their wives and children, according to our custom, but contrary to the custom of other tribes. [Campbell 1903:112]

Abortion was absent in the village of Tapouliang (Shang-tan-shui) (Chang Yao-ch'i 1951:6–7), two days' journey to the south (Campbell 1903:130, 157). In 1638 the missionaries reported:

> This village is very populous, much more so than the villages of Mattau and Soulang. . . . Abortion, which was formerly practised to a frightful extent in the northern villages, was not practised in Tapouliang. [Campbell 1903:163–164]

The 1650 census reports the following village populations: Tevorang, 971; Tapouliang, 1,874; Mattau, 1,411; and Soulang, 2,093 (Nakamura 1936:3, 5); this suggests that Tapouliang was not especially populous. The social organization of Tevorang and Tapouliang may have more closely approximated that of the Ami, who did not impose so extreme a delay on joint conjugal residence; see the discussion below.

20. I have already noted the ambiguity caused by the use of the pronoun "they" and that this passage may refer to infanticide rather than abortion.

21. The age grade systems of the Hsiu-ku-luan or central Ami and the coastal Ami were similar to that of the Nan-shih Ami, permitting marriage only after age 25 (Liu Pin-hsiung 1965:39; Yuan Chang-rue 1969:59, 119, 128, 144; on the Nan-shih Ami, see also Li Yi-yuan 1982:158–160).

22. Let us evaluate some of the alternative ways to delay family formation. Infanticide had many drawbacks compared to abortion. Infanticide can only occur after the mother endures the dangerous process of giving birth, and so massage abortion may well have been judged by the Siraya to entail less risk. Infanticide, unlike abortion, requires the mother to carry the child for a full nine months, imposing a heavy cost in energy and interfering with her ability to work in the fields. Avoiding a loss in agricultural labor power seems to me an unlikely explanation for the preference for abortion and the radical postponement of childbirth, however. Why should an optimal allocation of female labor power require agricultural labor from the young and very old, and childbearing only from the middle-aged? Would not a spacing out of childbearing be safer for maternal and infant health, and allow the same total input of labor in agriculture or hide processing? Fostering and adoption would allow a more efficient allocation of young female labor, for while not delaying childbearing, these solutions avoid both the fetal wastage of abortion and infancticide and the child-care burden (which is shifted to others), thereby enabling the young to delay family formation. Child care was undoubtedly shared by women of all ages (and even some men) in any case. After all, female agriculture is common to all Formosan aboriginal groups, and under much less affluent circumstances (described in the 20th-century ethnographies), women in these groups have had to accommodate pregnancies (and childrearing) to their work schedules without practicing abortion or infanticide. Abortion, especially in its extreme mandatory form, has no obvious advantages over these alternative means of delaying family formation, and it has many disadvantages.

There are yet other "funtional equivalents" (Hempel 1965; Sahlins 1976:77) that would have delayed families and avoided mandatory abortions, for example, abstinence and nonprocreative sex. We have already seen that abstinence would not have suited the Siraya.

5

Symbolic Analysis:
Sirayan Pregnancy Taboos in
Comparative and Historical Context

Having shown how mandatory abortion fits into a larger institutional pattern, let us probe further in this chapter to understand what cultural beliefs may have inspired these institutions, and, alternatively, in succeeding chapters what constellations of interest and power supported them.

Candidius provides us with very little information on how the Siraya represented the system of mandatory abortion to themselves. When Candidius exhorted the Siraya to abandon the practice of abortion, the women told him:

> "Our customs have been handed down to us from generation to generation and cannot be done away with." "Our priestesses, who are in daily converse with the spiritual world, know what is right and teach us accordingly." "Were we to disregard those priestesses, our gods would become angry, and would send no rain, but rather our foes, upon us, who would chase us from our country and destroy us." [Campbell 1903:95]

According to the women Candidius questioned, Siraya priestesses claimed that the gods themselves mandated abortion and warned that human disobedience would bring supernatural retribution in the form of drought and military defeat. If we couple these statements with the report that "[a]s long as the men go to war and generate children with their wives, they kill these children up to the time that they do not go to war any more" (Blusse and Roessingh 1984:70), we can see the Siraya positing a supernatural link between success in warfare and adherence to the rule of mandatory abortion for warriors' wives.[1]

Underlying this link is the opposition many Austronesian (and other) cultures postulate between female procreation and male head-hunting (or warring), between female life-giving and male life-taking (cf. Rosaldo and Atkinson 1975). Many cultures see in sexual intercourse and female reproductive processes (menstruation, childbirth, pregnancy) mysteries and dangers that must be hedged with taboos (cf. F. A. Hanson 1982). Many of these same cultures also see risks and supernatural dangers in male hunting and warfare. The Austronesian cultures of aboriginal Formosa are rich in examples of taboos linking these two themes.[2]

Let us review Formosan examples of such taboos, beginning with some general prohibitions restricting contact between male and female spheres of activity. Both the Tsou and the Ami forbid all female contact with men's hunting weapons (the taboo applies whether or not the woman is menstruating or pregnant), and in reciprocal fashion, male contact with women's farm implements and looms. The Tsou predict adverse consequences for the woman (or man) whose touch violates the taboo ("toucher liability," Wei Hui-lin et al. 1952:156; Ogawa 1990:86–87), while the Ami predict adverse consequences for the man whose weapons are touched ("touchee liability," Yamaji 1990:61; Huang Hsuan-wei 1988:20). Sexual relations between male and female may be polluting for either or both parties. David Wright reports that the Siraya forbade conjugal relations during the sacred period of *karichang,* predicting death for a husband who violated this taboo.[3] The Ami taboo sexual intercourse on a number of occasions: for both partners before important rituals, for men before entering the fields or going hunting or headhunting, and for women before opening their granaries (Wang Sung-hsing 1961:155, 166; Ting Hung-hsueh 1978:78, 80; Yamaji 1990:58, 61). Formosan groups as diverse as the Tsou, Bunun, Paiwan, Puyuma, and Ami taboo sexual intercourse before a headhunting expedition (Ho T'ing-jui 1956b:197 overleaf).

Beliefs that menstrual blood is dangerous and polluting to men are very widespread, and menstruating women are often subject to restrictions on their activities.[4] The Paiwan believe that contact with a menstruating woman will ruin a man's hunting; they prohibit menstruating and pregnant women from touching a man's weapons; and they forbid menstruating and pregnant women from participating in important rituals (Baudhuin 1960:493, 545, 467). The Rukai taboo even conversation with menstruating and pregnant women before a man joins a headhunting party (Ho T'ing-jui 1956b:197 overleaf). I know of no reports of menstrual huts or other requirements that menstruating women be secluded among Formosan groups, however. Ogawa specifically mentions that he found no elaboration of concepts of pollution in relation to menstruation among the Tsou (1990:100).

Contact with childbirth is also widely thought to be polluting for men. The Ami exclude husbands from the house during childbirth because they believe both that the presence of men will make labor difficult for the mother and that a father who comes into contact with the placenta of a newborn will meet misfortune in war and hunting (Liu Pin-hsiung 1965:113, 263; Yamaji 1990:58, 61). Thus the Ami encourage fathers to go hunting at the time of delivery, in order to avoid inauspicious contact with childbirth. The Puyuma and Atayal, on the other hand, do not exclude the husband from the house at the time of delivery, and deal with the danger of contact by confining the husband in the home and forbidding him hunting until the infant's umbilical cord dries and falls off (Yamaji 1990:xv; Kasahara 1986:44, 47). The Tsou also prohibit the father of the newborn from hunting and warfare (Wei Hui-lin et al. 1952:164).

Pregnancy is commonly believed to put both the mother and the father in a dangerous spiritual state and to create a mystical link between mother, unborn child, and father. A man's ability to fish, hunt, and fight may be adversely affected by his wife's pregnancy, and certain of his own actions may have magical consequences for his wife and child. The Ami impose a number of pregnancy taboos on expectant mothers and fathers: both members of the expecting couple are forbidden, for instance, to kill any animal "else their newborn may end up having warts like sword cuts" (Yamaji 1990:63). (Pregnancy taboos generally have the analogic form of sympathetic magic.)[5] Among the Ami a pregnant woman harms the crops if she enters the fields (Ting Hung-hsueh 1978:78), and her pregnancy renders ineffective the poison used by her husband in fishing (Sayama 1914:60). (This is true also of the Tsou; see Wei Hui-lin et al. 1952:157.) The Puyuma put a pregnant woman under the spiritual protection of a shamaness whose many prescriptions include requiring the husband to release bound objects and untie knots (thereby symbolically opening the birth passage) and to avoid funerals and death pollution (Kasahara 1986:42). The Paiwan considered it dangerous for a man whose wife was pregnant to join headhunting parties (Shih Lei 1971:164–65; Ho T'ing-jui 1956a:48) or attend funerals (T'ang Mei-chun 1973:11), forbade expectant fathers to kill animals lest it cause the fetus to die, and barred pregnant women from the fields (Matsuzawa 1986:16). Like the Paiwan, the Bunun and Saaroa forbade a man whose wife was pregnant from participating in headhunting; in addition, the Saaroa excluded an expectant father from ordinary hunting and from religious rituals (Baudhuin 1960:436, 444; Lin Pin-hsiung 1969:125).[6]

The danger a wife's pregnancy poses to her husband may also be linked to a related set of beliefs that the ghosts of women who die in childbirth seek revenge against their husbands. The belief that the death of a woman in childbirth is a bad death that produces an angry ghost, and requires special funerary treatment is reported for the Paiwan (T'ang Mei-chun 1973:27–28, 32–33), Ami (Bischofberger 1976:120), Puyuma (personal communication, Quack, 1993; Schroder 1967:30, 34), and Atayal (Kim 1980:225–226, 276), and for Austronesian groups beyond Taiwan (Blair and Robertson 1903:196; Lambrecht 1938:479–486; Sather 1978; Metcalf 1982:254–255).

In general, these taboos display in their formulation the following common logic. They posit two contrasting and mutually exclusive gender-linked spheres of activity: female procreation, on the one hand, and male hunting and warfare, on the other. Each sphere is in some way prototypical and unique to its corresponding gender, and each sphere is in part defined antithetically, that is, by what the other is not. Moreover, each set of activities is fraught with danger and potentially life-threatening. To ensure success in each sphere requires maintaining the difference by segregating the two spheres, exaggerating their opposition, and enforcing the division with reciprocal taboos. Successful performances in either sphere (safe delivery of a healthy child for women, victory in war for men) are threatened by contact with the contrasting sphere which contaminates, weakens, and endangers the performance. To achieve success requires separation of the two spheres to avoid contact that might transfer undesirable qualities from one sphere to the other. Taboos share with ritual magic their analogic form, but rather than seek an imperative transfer of desired qualities betweeen two spheres through contact, as in magic (Tambiah 1973), taboos operate to *prevent* the transfer of undesirable qualities by forbidding contact between two spheres. Note that these taboos operate to insulate, restrict, and polarize the activities of *both* partners, husband and wife, male and female, and not simply to devalue one gender vis-à-vis another.[7]

Our review of these taboos has established that beliefs that pregnancy and childbirth create spiritual danger for a woman's husband were very common among cognate tribes and neighbors of the Siraya, and among Austronesians generally.[8] It appears likely that the Siraya shared these beliefs and took an extreme view of the danger a wife's pregnancy posed for a headhunter in active age grade service (and perhaps of the danger a husband's headhunting posed for his pregnant wife and unborn child), just as they took an extreme position forbidding conjugal coresidence until the husband graduated from the age-grade ranks. For the Siraya, mandatory abortions for headhunters' wives would have minimized the dangers a wife's pregnancy posed for an active headhunter.

Note that these pregnancy taboos require abortion, rather than infanticide, in order to avoid the conflict between a man's headhunting duties to his age set and his procreative duties to his wife. For only abortion terminates the pregnancy that is the source of the danger for headhunters.[9] While I argue that pregnancy taboos were a necessary ingredient, I do not argue that they were in themselves sufficient to give rise to an institution like mandatory abortion. Many Formosan groups, after all, shared beliefs in pregnancy taboos without seeing any need to mandate abortions. In most Formosan groups it was sufficient for a man whose wife was pregnant simply to withdraw *temporarily* from head-hunting. Sirayan men and women were not given that option. Only among the Siraya were pregnancy taboos found in conjunction with extreme and prolonged demands for male age grade service.[10]

The problem posed by Sirayan mandatory abortion is to explain why *both* sets of beliefs *became* so extreme, compared to the Ami, for example. The ultimate answer, it seems to me, is in a complex historical process, a political economy of culture that links religious beliefs to social structure, and symbolic logics to institutions. Unfortunately, we can only speculate about Sirayan history before 1628, as it lies buried beyond our view and out of our reach. But that is all right so long as our analysis of Sirayan society has allowed for dynamics and we have been forced to recognize in Siraya society in the ethnographic present of 1628 an *historical* product. (We can, however, test this reconstruction against the events following 1628; see Chapter 7.)

The Siraya may well have believed that a man with a pregnant wife or a wife with children at home would not fight with the recklessness of a youth; indeed the Ami and Puyuma age-grade systems that postpone marriage and/or sex seem based on such beliefs.[11] Sirayan institutions may be seen as an extreme development of such beliefs: they radically postponed conjugal family life (but not sex) in favor of the warrior ideal and exclusive male age grade service. Supernatural sanctions, including those mandating abortion, helped maintain the system against the tensions it created between the demands of age-grade service and the pull of conjugal coresidence.

For his wife to bear children signified a headhunter's aging, his declining martial prowess, and his retirement; it also marked his transition from residence in the men's house and service to his natal family to residence with his wife's kin and on his wife's household's fields, and a transition in his productive role from hunting and headhunting to agriculture. In an institutional context where only retired men's wives bore children, a young woman who bore a child in violation of the rule of mandatory abortion would, by analogy, imply her husband's loss of youth and martial vigor, and might in this additional way (apart from the supernatural consequences attributed to violation of the taboo) have been believed to endanger his life in warfare.

The domestication of the headhunting male was marked symbolically when the retiring councillor caused "the hair on both sides of his forehead to be plucked out, which is a sign that he has fulfilled his term and is no longer in office" (Campbell 1903:15). The life stages of Siraya males (and the levels of libidinal aggressiveness expected at each stage) were symbolized by changes in hairdressing (Campbell 1903:15, 17–18).[12] The short hair of Siraya boys indicated immaturity and undeveloped sexuality, the long hair of headhunting males vigorous sexuality and aggressiveness, and the plucked temples of senior males restrained maturity and withdrawal from active age grade service.[13] For Siraya males childrearing came only upon graduation to senior status and was linked to an entire transformation in lifeway: a transition in residence, social relations, productive roles, and sexual access.

Notes

1. In the initial quotation cited in Chapter 1, Candidius reported "It would be considered a great shame, a great sin, if women bore any children before the age mentioned ..." (1903:20); but he does not specify in that passage any supernatural retribution.

2. The general lack in the historical record of Sirayan material in this area forces me to work largely by analogy with other Formosan and Austronesian cultures. I have elsewhere explored the theme of male-female oppositions in the context of Sirayan religion, and their operation in calendric rituals, see Shepherd 1986:29, 40. Figure 1 provides a map locating the Formosan groups referred to below.

3. The third commandment reads "No Married-men shall sleep with their Wives in the time of Karichang, neither shall a Young Man espouse, nor bring his Household-stuff or Goods to his Bride, nor enjoy her, lest he die soon after, have a lingring Sickness, or live at debate." (Wright in Shepherd 1986:75).

4. These beliefs are by no means universal, however, and when they do appear they take a variety of culturally determined forms, see Buckley and Gottlieb 1988.

5. The Ami posit a mystical relation between a husband and wife even in the absence of pregnancy; thus a wife is forbidden to weave when her husband is out hunting as "should her yarns become entangled, an accident would almost certainly occur in the mountains," (Yamaji 1990:61). On the analogic form of taboos generally, see Tambiah 1973.

6. The Saisiat also believed a wife's pregnancy interfered with her husband's hunting (Baudhuin 1960:482). I find it intriguing that the Saaroa term for pregnancy, *paliali*, is a cognate of the word for taboo, *palisi*, a feature that Saaroa shares with Saisiat and the Philippine languages, Cebuano and Tagalog (Tsuchida 1988:25).

7. Wei Hui-lin et al. 1952:156 provides an early discussion of reciprocal sex-linked taboos among the Tsou. These themes are explored for Austronesian cultures outside Taiwan by Rosaldo and Atkinson 1975, Hanson 1982, Valeri 1990, and Atkinson 1990. Valeri (1990:257 ff.), following Rosaldo and Atkinson's early formulation (1975:70), employs male:female::culture:nature logic to contrast volitional headhunting to nonvolitional (and therefore devalued) childbirth. Contrary to Valeri's assumptions, the widespread practice of abortion among Austronesians (see the notes on Philippine practice below) suggests that childbirth is conceived to be volitional (accord Atkinson 1990:71). See Paige and

Paige 1981:34–41 for a critical review of psychological and other theories that attempt to account for couvade and pregnancy restrictions.

8. There are many examples of other Austronesian societies that posit mystical connections between husband, expectant wife, and fetus. Some reports stress danger for the husband, others for the unborn child and wife. Reports from several groups indicate that husbands are prohibited from taking life during a wife's pregnancy (St. John 1863:170; Skeat 1900:349; Barton 1938:208; Borneo Literature Bureau 1963:52; Endicott 1970:59, 73; Laderman 1983:91). Other groups apply different restrictions to the activities of expectant husbands (Roth 1893:207–212; Garvan 1929:111–112; Evans 1953:87–88; Scharer 1963:85), and even where explicit taboos are absent, as in Tikopia, Firth reports that "the pregnancy of a woman tends to rob her husband of efficacy or success in his everyday pursuits," (1967:35–36). Women are also called on to observe taboos while men are off headhunting (Rutter 1929:190–91; Barton 1938:168; Borneo Literature Bureau 1963:59–62). Davison and Sutlive note that the Iban observe reciprocal taboos, husbands for pregnant wives and wives for warrior husbands, and that men killed in battle and women who die in childbirth go to a special place in the Iban afterworld (1991:194). Hose and McDougall report the Kayan believed that in the afterlife women who died in childbirth became the wives of men who died violent deaths (1912:40, 155–156). Cultures as divergent as the Thai and the Aztecs also posit a complementarity between the dangers of warfare for men and childbirth for women (Caso 1958:13, 58–59; Tambiah 1970:315).

9. The identification of the pregnancy stage as a period of danger for husband and unborn child contrasts with the couvade customs of South America. There it is the birth, rather than the pregnancy, that initiates the period of greatest mystical danger for the child and necessitates the imposition of severe restrictions on the behavior of the parents (Fock 1967; Maybury-Lewis 1967:65ff.). The differences in timing are related to differences in conceptions of when soul-attachment and other developmental stages occur and are most vulnerable to disturbance.

10. Nor would I argue that the practice of massage abortion could only occur where male age grade organizations made extreme demands on husbands, for massage abortion was widespread among Austronesians. I do note, however, that only the Siraya are reported to have *mandated* abortion.

11. Fuller notes uses of this logic to explain the Nayar pattern of marriage and duolocal residence (1976:5).

12. Head hair is used to symbolize libidinal aggressiveness and vital power in many cultures and changes in hairdressing frequently signal changes in sexual status (Leach 1958:153–154). That hair symbolized libidinal potency for Siraya is further indicated by the magical power they attributed to hair separated from the heads of their foes; such hair they braided and hung about the altars where trophy skulls were displayed (Blusse and Roessingh 1984:70, 75; cf. Leach 1958:158). Iban headhunters were entitled to a special coiffure, and decorated the hilts of headhunting swords with human hair (Davison and Sutlive 1991:157, 180). Compare also the Saluan of Sulawesi (Ishii 1990:202–204).

13. Gender restrictions vary with age and life-cycle stage, as well as by activity and social relationship (e.g., marriage ties, household membership). It is often noted that sex-linked taboos are relaxed for postmenopausal women; less noted is that they may also be relaxed for older men. Among the Tsou, elderly men who no longer go hunting are free to weave the basket carried by

every woman, and to hold an infant girl; both acts would be avoided by active hunters (Ogawa 1990:87, 89). Young preadolescent boys who have not begun to stay at a men's house may also do women's work of feeding pigs (Ogawa 1990:78, 100). Liu Pin-hsiung suggests the Saaroa lift similar restrictions on men above age forty (1969:121). This underlines the link of taboo systems to gender-typical activities and not to biological identity.

6

Complementary Perspectives

I have now laid out my reconstruction of Sirayan mandatory abortion, based on an interpretation that is both institutional and symbolic. Both age grade strictures and pregnancy taboos appear to have become particularly extreme in the course of Sirayan history, compared to the Ami and other Formosan groups, and resulted in the mandating of abortion for headhunters' wives. But this is not the only interpretation that is possible, or that has been proposed. I turn in this section to evaluate some of these complementary perspectives for the light they may shed on our problem (also see Appendix A for a Freudian perspective), before turning in the following section to examine whether events after 1628 are consistent with my reconstruction.

Gendered Perspectives

The analysis so far has sought an answer to the meaning of mandatory abortion by shifting focus: the role of pregnant women and priestesses has been pushed to the background while the construction of the larger Sirayan social and cultural order, and especially the role of male age grade organization, has been brought into the foreground. In making this shift of focus, have we fallen into the pitfalls of androcentric models of society? To avoid this trap, we must test against the Sirayan data interpretations of mandatory abortion suggested by feminist points of view that focus on women as societal agents, not merely as passive victims. We must ask what "benefits" mandatory abortion may have had for young women and old priestesses in order to understand what motivated their compliance with mandatory abortion. Let us begin by considering young women's points of view.

Childbirth can be frightening and dangerous for women; mandatory abortion gave young Sirayan women a means of postponing this life-threatening event (albeit at the expense of undergoing painful massage abortions that were not risk free). Compared to women in patriarchal societies who must bear children early and often to gain a secure status in their husbands' families, Sirayan women were born into and passed their lives in matrifocal families where their status did not depend on producing children and heirs. Nor, apparently, were the

Siraya suffering from the high rates of infant mortality which make frequent childbearing necessary, or the poverty that counsels parental investment in many children in the anticipation of the economic payback they will make.[1]

Freedom from childbearing and rearing due to abortions must have eased the burdens Sirayan agricultural practices and the gender division of labor placed on young women. It must also have given them greater freedom and opportunity to conduct love affairs with a number of men. Mandatory abortion prolonged this period of a woman's life.[2] We have already seen that divorce was easy and adultery commonplace among the Siraya, suggesting that love affairs were among the pleasures of Sirayan youth (Campbell 1903:20). Candidius reports:

> They declare—when I have rebuked them for fornication—that their gods find pleasure in it. Hence, when parents know that their children commit fornication, provided it be not done in public, they laugh about it and do not forbid it. [Campbell 1903:24]

Sirayan women may also have disliked childbirth because it ruined youthful figures and sex appeal (cf. Devereux 1976:126ff.).

Candidius's earliest account of mandatory abortion dated August 20, 1628, carries the suggestion that the women saw certain advantages to the practice:

> This crime of destroying the fruit of the womb is committed by the women till they have reached their thirtieth, thirty-third, or thirty-fifth year. They also feel *proud* of the number of children they have destroyed; several women having confessed to me that they had already killed eight, others twelve, and others again fifteen. Their priestesses teach them that it would be a shame for them not to act in this way; these old crones being the very ones who are called in by expectant mothers to procure abortion. [Campbell 1903:95, emphasis added]

In this passage Candidius implies that women actively sought abortions from the priestesses (Sirayan women no doubt understood that the earlier the fetus was aborted, the less painful and dangerous the procedure would be) and that they even took pride in the number of their abortions. Sirayan women might well take pride in frequent pregnancies that offered proof of their fecundity, sexual attractiveness, and success in love affairs, while abortions eliminated the burden of childrearing.[3] But mandatory abortion was not necessary to perpetuate the freedom of adolescence. Infanticide and adoption, in addition to abortion, could also free girls from the duties of motherhood, and did so in many Polynesian cultures (Ortner 1981:385). For Siraya, prolonged adolescence, then, is more a consequence than a cause of mandatory abortion.

Perhaps Sirayan women, disgusted by the behavior of young men who came around only for sex, who contributed little to agricultural production, and who spent the bulk of their time with their male comrades in sport, the hunt, and warfare, were refusing to bear children until the men survived their warrior years, settled down, began to contribute to agriculture, and could share the burdens of farming and child rearing. It is possible to read the report of the Constant and Pessaert expedition in just this way: "As long as the men go to war and generate children with their wives, they kill these children up to the time that they do not go to war any more" (Blusse and Roessingh 1984:70). The Siraya system of marriage delayed childrearing until it could take place in the context of conjugal coresidence. Thus women may well have preferred abortion despite its costs, as long as their husbands were barred from taking up permanent uxorilocal residence. This interpretation receives support from the analysis of Dutch efforts to abolish abortion presented in Chapter 7, where we see that, when men were freed from the age grade ban on conjugal coresidence, the women seem quite willingly to have abandoned abortion.

Mandatory abortion, therefore, had advantages for young women, but we should not forget that this was an institution dictating that women abort, rather than an institution leaving it to individual women to decide when to have children and thereby increasing women's control over their own fertility. The Siraya practiced *mandatory* abortion, not choice. Because the advantages abortion conferred on women could have been attained by practices less extreme than mandatory abortion (e.g., spacing births, fostering), I do not see the institution as a response to women's interests, though it certainly accommodated them to some extent.[4] What distinguishes the Siraya from a very similar group like the Ami where female agriculture and matrifocal households operated without abortion is the extreme development of the Siraya age grade system (and the greater affluence of the 17th century).[5]

While abortion extended a carefree period of youth for Sirayan women, they may have felt that abortion to age 30 or 35 *over*extended this period, for mandatory abortion also deprived women of the ability to start families, kept young women subordinated to senior women and priestesses, and deprived them of the full adult status that comes with parenthood. Thus we will see below that when the Dutch abolished duolocal residence and abortion they met with a generally positive reaction from Sirayan youth.

Elderly priestesses figure prominently in Candidius's description of abortion: both as teachers of the principles that mandated abortion and as the masseuses that induced abortions. As we shall see below, these priestesses, or *inibs*, were a major obstacle to Dutch missionary success. Candidius's description of Sirayan society attributes great authority to these senior women, and we may well ask what the basis for this influence was and how it related to the institution of mandatory abortion.[6] Candidius asserts that all religious observances were in the priestesses' hands and that there were no male ritual specialists, although he qualifies this somewhat when he notes that the gods who confer success in war "are most worshipped and served by the men," (Campbell 1903:24). Wright's description confirms that priestesses played the prominent role in all public celebrations (Shepherd 1986: 69 ff.). Priestesses addressed prayers to the gods, offered sacrifices, served as vehicles of shamanistic possession, and conducted exorcisms (Campbell 1903:24–25).

The high status of women in religion and ritual was matched by high status among the gods. A goddess, along with her husband, stood at the head of the Sirayan pantheon. Her marriage implies she was sexually active, and significantly, no children are mentioned (Campbell 1903:24; also Wright in Shepherd 1986:71). This was no idealized mother goddess but a woman whose voice is described as the thunder, chiding her husband for not sending rain (Campbell 1903:24).[7] This divine couple controlled the fertility of the crops, and it was primarily women who presented them offerings to ensure rain and good harvests (Campbell 1903:24; Shepherd 1986:71–72).

The prominence accorded goddesses and priestesses (and agriculture) in the religious sphere was matched by the autonomy and high status accorded Sirayan women generally.[8] We have already noted that women possessed their own fields and houses and enjoyed considerable authority in matrifocal households. Marriages were easily terminated, created few claims to wifely property or labor, and put little restriction on women's sexual and other activities. The male constitution of villagewide leadership in the men's houses appears to have intruded little into these spheres of female activity.

Secular leadership was in the hands of the councillors who ranked at the top of the male age grades. Their formal authority was limited to the imposition of fines for public infractions. Important issues were decided in male deliberative assemblies (Campbell 1903:15–16) while people wronged by acts of theft, manslaughter, and adultery were left to seek compensation through self-help (Campbell 1903:16–17). In religious matters the secular leaders were required to heed the instructions of the *inibs*; thus Candidius reports that it is "part of a councillor's office to see that the commands of their priestesses are duly obeyed, and to prevent everything that they fancy may provoke the anger of the gods" (Campbell 1903:15). The prominent role of senior women in the religious sphere reinforced women's independence in the agricultural and household spheres and limited attempts to extend male dominance. The complementarity of female spiritual and male secular power is a widespread theme among Austronesian cultures (Mabuchi 1974; Hoskins 1988).

Sirayan society appears then to have been built around largely separate but complementary male and female spheres in which each gender enjoyed considerable autonomy. The religious power of the priestesses must have reinforced the dominance of senior over junior women within the female sphere, just as the system of age grades subordinated junior to senior males. Thus it was from a position of considerable influence that the priestesses mandated abortion for young women.[9] Yet it remains unclear whether we can properly describe mandatory abortion as coercive. Was it any more coercive than male subjection to age grade discipline, or any number of customary practices (tattooing, tooth extraction, initiatory hazing, etc.) that inflict pain, to be sure, but whose subjects accept the pain as the cost of achieving a valued social attribute? There is no suggestion in the sources that mandatory abortion served the "interests" of the senior women or that the priestesses mandated abortion at the behest of senior males. We may speculate (without evidence) that in mandating abortions postmenopausal priestesses were motivated by jealousy of the fecundity of young women or by material interest aimed at maximizing ritual fees and/or female agricultural labor,[10] or even that they were championing the rights of young women against the demands of men for more children. The explanations of abortion which the young women gave to Candidius suggest rather that young (and old) women were acting out a shared model of the female life cycle and its (sometimes mystical) relation to the male life cycle, not that they felt exploited by their seniors.

Sirayan society mandated abortion for its young women in the same way it mandated age grade service for its young men; both institutions were compulsory, and neither reflected in any direct way the "interests" of the groups most affected. Sirayan society expected young women to give priority not to marriage and childrearing but to horticulture and love affairs, in the same way that it expected young men to pursue hunting, headhunting, and lovers. Childrearing was delayed until husband and wife were permitted to take up residence together. These culturally formed styles of life had costs as well as benefits, but they were reproduced by individuals whose goals and values were formed by the overall structure of Sirayan social organization, not by individuals making choices in a cultural and social vacuum. That they were historical products and subject to change we shall see below.

The Demand for Children

I argued above that there is no evidence that the Siraya population was outgrowing its resources or that mandatory abortion had been adopted in response to demographic pressure, although there can be no doubt that mandatory abortion had as a consequence the limiting of population growth. But now that we understand how Sirayan institutions of marriage and family operated, we may consider whether these institutions made the Siraya disinterested in population growth and therefore tolerant of abortion. The Siraya may in certain senses have felt their village populations were already large enough, thereby reducing any desire on their part to push for population growth by overturning the rules on mandatory abortion.

From the men's point of view, we may postulate several reasons why they would not press for increased numbers of children: (i) a larger population would increase the distance they had to travel between their natal households and the residences of their wives;[11] (ii) an even larger village might become unwieldy to manage and maintaining internal peace might become more difficult; (iii) the villages were already large enough to field sufficient military force to provide for defense; and (iv) more children might reduce female labor in the fields and increase pressure on men to engage in despised agricultural labor.

Nor should we expect Sirayan women to press for more children. Mandatory abortion freed young women from the burdens of childbirth and childrearing (and may have given them a relatively carefree life and the freedom to take lovers), and it is likely that uxorilocal marriage enabled them to retain some control over their own fertility even after their husbands took up joint residence.

While we need not assume that both men and women accepted unquestioningly the system of duolocal residence and abortion, it nevertheless appears that neither the interests of the women or the men were such as would lead them to push for increased numbers of children in opposition to the teachings of the priestesses. The affluence and good health of the Sirayan population made it possible for the Siraya to bear and rear large numbers of children at the same time it made it unnecessary. Neither Sirayan men nor women, from their respective institutional positions, had any particular interest in pressing for more children.

The preceding discussion clearly supposes that Siraya individuals have interests and motives that, while culturally formed, do not simply reflect the publicly enunciated cultural norms of their society. This contrasts with symbolic analyses of cultural representations that suffer from an oversocialized conception of human actors and never question the degree to which actors subscribe to hegemonic cultural representations (cf. Wrong 1961; Barth 1987). The integrated systems of symbols and meanings posited by symbolic analyses provide no means for understanding why societies change over time (as in functionalist and consensus sociology, change can only come from outside the system), nor can they explain why deviance and structures enforcing conformity to norms exist in every society. Anthropological analysis must comprehend actions and norms, as well as the representations that are the selective focus of interpretivists (cf. Holy and Stuchlik 1983). Cultural interpretation divorced from analysis of social action and historical dynamics produces thin, not thick, descriptions. Conflict theories of society that see individuals as historical actors (as well as historical products) and social and cultural formations as continously open to historical change avoid these errors (cf. Dahrendorf 1968). Conflict theory sees in any cultural and institutional formation the product of a differential distribution of the burdens as well as the benefits of power, privilege, and status; any social formation thus carries within it dynamic tensions that generate change over time. In the next chapter we turn to an historical account of the demise of Sirayan mandatory abortion that reveals some of the political dynamics shaping the Sirayan social order.

Notes

1. Compare the equally affluent Visayan (Philippine) women who are reported in this passage from a late-16th-century source to have used massage abortion to space children and limit fertility:

> Women dislike to give birth many times, specially those who inhabit the towns near the sea, saying that in having many children they are like pigs, for which reason after having one or two [children] the next time they get pregnant, when they are already three or four months [with child], they kill the creature in their body and abort. There are women for this calling and by massaging the stomach and placing certain herbs the creature later dies and the pregnant woman aborts. [Quirino and Garcia 1958:413]

This description of massage abortion resembles those for the Siraya reported in Chapter 1. Sirayan women, who were required to delay childbearing for so long, were, however, less likely to be interested in using massage abortions to *space* births.

2. On Yap some young women enjoyed love affairs and delayed childbearing until age 30 through self-induced abortions (Schneider 1968:393). Indeed, Yapese young women aborted despite a generally shared perception that Yap was underpopulated and a male view that considered abortion immoral (Schneider 1968:383–384; Devereux 1976:353–354). (For questions about Schneider's claims as to the frequency of abortions, however, see Chapter 3, note 13.)

3. Serbians, for example, consider sterility and childlessness a tragedy for women (who could be divorced on such grounds), while at the same time they seek consciously to limit family size. Thus Morokvasic reports the following attitudes among Serbian women:

> Though abortion is the opposite of procreation, it is symbolically the same—physical proof that a woman is fecund. Among older women the number of their abortions is a matter of pride. . . . Yugoslav women are very proud of their sexual drive. . . . Abortion . . . permit[s] the capacity to procreate to be tested while ensuring the control of fertility. [1984:204–205]

High frequencies of abortion are reported for Serbia throughout the 20th century; the traditional methods were abdominal massage assisted by midwives and abortifacients (Morokvasic 1984:196; Halpern 1958:201–202).

4. It is worth noting here that maternal mortality rates increase steadily for women after age 30 (Dunn 1949:XL), a point that suggests women would prefer to bear their desired children earlier in life.

5. By the 20th century the deer herds had been long depleted, and the no-longer-affluent Formosan aborigines were living primarily on marginal land. In 1933 aborigines on the average (the Ami are near the norm) had a low life expectancy, a crude death rate of 34 per thousand, and a crude birth rate of 45 per thousand, which requires that women bear approximately six children each if a stable population is to be maintained (Wang Jen-ying 1967:113; Coale 1974:44–45).

6. Female magicians and shamans play prominent roles in nearly all the other Formosan groups, but they rarely dominate the religious sphere to the exclusion of male priests. Among the Ami, portions of the millet harvest ritual require exclusive female officiation (Ting Hung-hsueh 1978a:82), but male priests provide overall ritual leadership.

Both female religious leadership and abortion by massage are reported among the cultures of the nearby Philippines. Priestesses and female shamans play leading ritual roles in northern Luzon (F. Keesing 1962:317, also 57–58, 187–191) and in several Mindanao cultures (e.g., Cole 1913:62–63, 100–101; Garvan 1929:209–210). There is also widespread among Philippine cultures a tradition of midwifery which uses massage as a central technique (Cole 1913:100–101; Garvan 1929:113; Hart 1965:18–22, 32–33, 55–56; for cases beyond the Philippines see Lee 1972:35–36; Laderman 1983:115); these midwife/masseuses are often known to be able to procure abortion by massaging the abdomen (Yu and Liu 1980:135–39). For notices of the widespread use of a variety of abortion techniques in Philippine cultures, including massage abortion, see Pedrosa 1983, and Chapter 1, note 9. Many of these cultures employ massage as a general curing technique (Hart 1965:21–22; Yu and Liu 1980:123). Massage is alluded to in reports on Formosan groups (Wu Yen-ho 1965:121; Schroder 1967:28; Benedek 1987:161), and its use by Sirayan priestesses to cure illness is condemned in a sermon by the missionary Junius (Campbell 1903:334). These cultures thus combined in various permutations the roles of priestess, healer-masseuse, midwife, and abortionist.

7. The Ami also have a husband-wife pair of gods whose domestic rows cause thunder and lightning. The husband by knocking about the household effects, causes thunder, and the wife, by uncovering herself, gives origin to lightning (Myers 1884:44).

8. The Siraya assigned to women the chief responsibility for mourning the dead (Campbell 1903:22; Wright 1671:29–30 in Shepherd 1986:67–68). This would contradict high female status if we follow the interpretation linking female mourning to death and decay (Bloch and Parry 1982:21 ff., 215, 226, but see Martin 1988), but not if we follow interpretations linking female mourning to vitality (Huntington and Metcalf 1979:101ff.).

9. The Siraya case would give more support to a "sororal interest group theory" than to the Paiges' "fraternal interest group theory" of reproductive rituals. The Paiges hypothesize that societies with strong fraternal interest groups maintain "ritual surveillance" over pregnant women; they interpret the labeling of pregnant women as dangerous, and abortions in cases of uncertain paternity, as examples of such ritual surveillance (Paige and Paige 1981:179, 185). The Siraya case contradicts the Paiges' theory; the matrifocal Siraya, despite their lack of fraternal interest groups, saw dangers in pregnant women and practiced abortion anyway (although not for reasons of uncertainty of paternity).

10. The priestesses are reported collecting fees for massage cures and abortions (Campbell 1903:182–183, 334).

11. Soulang was already so large that some of the men had to walk a quarter to half an hour in the dark to reach their wives' residences (Blusse and Roessingh 1984:69).

7

The Abolition of Abortion under Dutch Rule

From the beginning of their presence on the island the Dutch missionaries campaigned to abolish abortion and foster conjugal coresidence and family life. Missionary efforts and Dutch rule had profound effects on the Siraya system of marriage and abortion, but only after the Dutch East India Company launched a major campaign of pacification in 1635. Analysis of the timing and nature of the Siraya response to Dutch reform efforts enables us to test our reconstruction of a Sirayan society practicing mandatory abortion and delayed transfer uxorilocal marriage against the record of events after 1628.

The Dutch clergy denounced as immoral both duolocal residence and abortion and advocated its own conception of companionate marriage and patriarchal family. The missionaries preached against abortion (and priestesses) and encouraged married couples to live and work together and rear children jointly (Campbell 1903:162, 182–183, 186). The catechisms composed by Candidius's colleague and successor Reverend Junius (active 1629–43) taught that abortion violated the Sixth Commandment against taking of life, condemned adultery, and enjoined marriage on all believers (Campbell 1903:338, 347, 371).

By as early as 1636 the missionaries had married more than fifty couples from the village of Sinkan according to Dutch rites (Campbell 1903:143). By 1639 that number had risen to 119 couples out of a Sinkan population reported to total 1,047 souls (all baptized), including 154 men able to bear arms (Campbell 1903:179). This is a substantial number of marriages. Since it appears that the missionaries were marrying only younger couples living duolocally (and not older couples already living jointly)[1] and that men able to bear arms were those between 20 and 35 years of age (the definition of "grown-up men" for purposes of church schooling; see Campbell 1903:225), the 119 couples represents a very high proportion of men of marriageable age in the village of Sinkan. As couples married in the Dutch fashion were expected to take up joint residence (which remained uxorilocal) and not to practice abortion (as the passages cited below indicate), the large number of couples so married indicates a rather impressive willingness and ability on the part

58

of the Sinkan Siraya to accept the Dutch redefinition of their marriage institutions. We need to explain why.

The willingness of the Sinkan Siraya to marry in the Dutch fashion grew with each Dutch military victory and can be explained as a result of the transformation of the Sinkan political environment and religious worldview. In expanding their colonial realm by force of arms in 1635 and 1636, the Dutch made allies of the Sinkan Siraya, who thereby shared in Dutch victories. This sudden improvement in the politico-military situation of Sinkan disrupted the traditional bases of authority in the village, for as the Dutch imposed peace among the villages, they deprived the age-grade hierarchies of the most important justification of their existence: defense and glory in warfare. The Dutch peace also opened the way to a restructuring of the Sirayan world view by challenging the supernatural ties that linked military service in age grades for young husbands to mandatory abortion and separate residence for young wives.

A brief review of Sirayan political history under the Dutch is necessary to see this dynamic at work.[2] Although the Dutch did not initially seek to extend their territorial control beyond the port of Tayouan, they found it difficult not to become involved in intervillage strife in the hinterland. Thus, not long after their arrival the Dutch sent a "hundred musketeers" to deliver Sinkan from its enemies, the neighboring villages of Mattau and Bakloan (Campbell 1903:96). This early alliance between the Dutch and Sinkan accounts for Sinkan's tolerance of Candidius's presence in the village. The Dutch garrison, however, remained undermanned, and the Dutch inability to punish the slaughter of a Dutch force by Mattau in 1629 was a great blow to Dutch prestige. Finally in 1631 the Dutch, joined by the Sinkandians, launched small but successful raids on Mattau and a southern village, Tampsui. Governor Putmans gives this account of the expedition's results:

> In this expedition the people of Sinkan captured one head only. Three or four men of Tampsui were also shot down, but the foe immediately dragged the corpses into the high grass and jungle, so that the heads of the fallen enemy could not be captured. The results of the expedition are satisfactory; for the minds of the people of Sinkan have been so favourably turned to us that the whole village shows an inclination to adopt our religion. Some of the principal men—and it is to these that the other inhabitants chiefly look—have cast away their idols, and are being daily instructed by Candidius. [Campbell 1903:102–103]

Mattau was causing trouble again in 1633, but it was not until August 1635 that the Dutch garrison was reinforced by the arrival of four hundred soldiers. In November 1635 a Dutch force, joined by Sinkandian allies, attacked Mattau, and set the village afire. Within days Mattau sent representatives to sue for peace (Campbell 1903:109, 117–119). In December 1635 the Dutch and Sinkandians marched south to punish villages there for some murders of Dutch and Sinkandians, and in January 1636 they marched north to punish Soulang. At Soulang the Dutch demanded that the villagers themselves hand over those responsible for crimes against the Dutch; in the face of overwhelmingly superior force, Soulang complied. The Dutch then delivered the Soulang prisoners to the Sinkandians for decapitation, in order "to unite" the Sinkandians to the Dutch (Campbell 1903:121, 123–126).

This series of Dutch victories sent shock waves throughout the region and shattered local power balances. The Sinkandians, puffed up by their victories, began spreading rumors and making threats against their rivals (Campbell 1903:122, 152). Throughout January 1636 villages from all over the region sued for peace. By August 1636, 57 villages had submitted to the Dutch (Campbell 1903:140). It was in this radically transformed political environment that the Sinkandians began to accept the teachings of the Dutch missionaries.

In 1628, before the Dutch had demonstrated their military power, the Sinkandians had been quite skeptical of Candidius's teachings, even suspecting that the Dutch "endeavour to estrange them from their religion, in order that their gods may become angry with them," (Campbell 1903:95). The Sinkandians therefore proposed practical experiments to test the validity of Christian teachings, as Candidius reports:

> [T]hey have proposed that I should begin by giving Christian instruction in one house only, and that all its inmates should abandon their manners and customs and adopt ours. If their gods still continued to bless that house by giving much rice and other things during the next two or three years, they too would willingly adopt our religion. They also come to me to test my powers, asking me to perform miracles, to give or withhold rain and wind, to foretell future events, or to reveal what is actually occurring elsewhere; and because I cannot do so, they despise me, and say that their priestesses can do all such things. [Campbell 1903:95–96][3]

The victories of 1635 and 1636 brought a marked improvement in Sinkandian attitudes toward the Dutch and missionary teachings. In late 1636 we are told of the Sinkandians:

> The people are very much inclined to wage war, not only on account of the honour they may thereby acquire, but also for the sake of booty. . . . So eager are they to obtain booty that, when we even hint our intention of marching against a village, they are immediately ready to set out on a long expedition or attack their immediate neighbours, as they did in the case of Mattau and Soulang. [Campbell 1903:152]

The Dutch thereby provided the means by which Sinkandians could succeed in achieving their traditional military aspirations. Governor van der Burg, after his visit to Sinkan on October 24, 1636, reported:

> It is impossible for me to refrain from praising the docility and tractability of these folk; . . . so ready to wage war against our enemies, and so willing to be taught by Mr. Junius the doctrines of the Christian faith. [Campbell 1903:152]

The Sinkandians were discovering new supernatural routes to victory in war. The god of the Dutchmen brought victory over their enemies, and the Sinkandian gods had failed to take revenge on those who had forsaken them. In September 1636 the Reverend Junius filed this report:

> As to the two large villages of Mattau and Soulang, we do not doubt that it would be an easy task to persuade their inhabitants to renounce idolatry, the more so as they see the prosperity of Sinkan, where the people began many years ago to serve the true God, and whose crops of rice every one sees to be plentiful, being abundant year after year and promising now to be as plentiful as ever. This test is looked upon as being of great importance by the inhabitants of Formosa. Many old persons in Sinkan, especially among the former priestesses, ventured to prophesy to the people at the time of their conversion that, if they neglected their idols and began to serve the God of the Dutchmen, their fields would no longer yield them their crops of rice. Not only, however, have they seen that the contrary has happened, but that the crops have been much more abundant than before their conversion. This fact has seriously interfered with the native forms of worship, so much that the people themselves now laugh at their priestesses, whose words were formerly received as oracles, and were believed with the same certainty and conviction which we have as regards the Gospel. [Campbell 1903:139–140]

Thus the old religion had been discredited; both abundant harvests and victories in war had disproved the claims of the priestesses. The god of the Dutchmen, who had so amply demonstrated his power, did not require that married couples postpone joint residence and the rearing of children as a condition of his favors; on the contrary, his missionaries actively preached against abortion and in favor of conjugal coresidence. Success in war no longer depended on headhunters living in men's houses with their age-mates, separated from their wives, or on head-hunters' wives aborting their pregnancies. That so many (119) Sinkan couples had remarried in the Dutch fashion by 1639 suggests that there was little opposition to this change and, indeed, that young couples may have welcomed it.

Young Sinkandian husbands and wives, freed from mandatory abortion and the prohibition on conjugal coresidence, were able to establish (uxorilocal) conjugal families earlier than ever before. In 1639

Commissioner Couckebacker recorded the progress achieved by the missionaries in Sinkan against the custom of abortion and duolocal residence and linked that progress to the discrediting of the old religion:

> In Sinkan, one hundred and nineteen couples have been married according to our rites, and live together in a godly manner. The young women no longer practise abortion, and their priestesses are now as much despised as they were formerly honoured; for it is now seen how they used to extort the villagers' possessions under the pretext of serving their idols. [Campbell 1903:182–183]

Discussing Sinkan in October 1640, Junius reports that young husbands and wives were working together in the fields, bearing children and coresiding:

> To our surprise, we daily see young people there not only marrying according to Christian rites, going together into the fields, and bringing children into the world, but even living together, while formerly they would rather have died than live thus. Even in Mr. Candidius' time, it appeared almost impossible to bring all this about. More and more their former customs and manners are disappearing, and they are conforming to our ways. [Campbell 1903:186]

The events that had transformed the world view of the Sinkandians in Junius's time and made possible conjugal families were of course the victories of 1635 and 1636. Thus the combined effect of Dutch-imposed political hegemony and the teachings of the missionaries was to subvert the extreme strictures of male age grade service and the religion of the priestesses; by weakening the institutions that forced the postponement of joint postmarital residence and childbearing, the scales were tipped in favor of the early formation of uxorilocal families.[4]

    In the neighboring villages both the demonstration effect of continuing good harvests in Sinkan and defeat at the hands of the Dutch undermined the authority of priestesses and age grade councillors. In these cases the missionary effort could rely on growing Dutch political hegemony to guarantee receptivity to its program, including the abolition of mandatory abortion. Thus when the Dutch governor and 75 bodyguards came to Soulang on a tour of inspection in February 1638, the chiefs of Soulang, after hearing a sermon from Junius, were moved to declare to the Dutch:

> that from henceforth the people were to desist from all lewdness and fornication; that the women when pregnant should no longer practise abortion; and that polygamy, which is most shamefully practised, should be done away with. Further, that the men should cover their nakedness, and henceforth live as Christians and not as beasts. [Campbell 1903:162]

In villages where they exercised political control the Dutch punished violations of these tenets that came to their attention. In 1642 the Dutch executed three residents of Soulang in a case apparently involving infanticide rather than abortion (Campbell 1903:189).

Missionary influence grew along with the consolidation of the new Dutch order. So confident were the Dutch of their political position that in 1641 they expelled 250 priestesses from at least five Sirayan villages, thereby removing their chief spiritual competitors (Campbell 1903:288–289). By 1643 Junius claimed to have baptized 5,400 persons and married more than one thousand couples in six Sirayan villages (1903:193).[5]

Under Dutch rule young Siraya were able to achieve the traditional ideal of conjugal coresidence earlier than ever before. The missionaries assumed the willingness of the Siraya to marry in the Dutch fashion reflected Sirayan acceptance of Christian doctrines and values. Given our understanding of the structured dynamics of Sirayan society, a better view of the impact of the Dutch is to see them offering to the Siraya not new values but new routes to the achievement of traditional Sirayan values: military alliances that yielded unprecedented victories (despite violation of the strictures of the priestesses); village security guaranteed by intervillage peace (instead of intervillage warfare); marriages that enabled young Siraya to achieve earlier than ever before their traditional ideal of (uxorilocal) conjugal coresidence and parenthood; and, also for the young, full social adulthood free of the domination of senior males and priestesses, and the burdens of extreme age grade regimentation and mandatory abortion.[6]

Thus this historical episode reveals that age grade hierarchy, pregnancy taboos, and mandatory abortion formed a complex dependent on a political structure of authority in Siraya villages. When that political structure and the ideology sustaining it were challenged by the Dutch, Siraya youth proved willing to reject the authority of their seniors and risk violating traditional taboos to marry and bear children according to Dutch rules rather than Siraya ones.

The history of this period reveals that to be successful the missionaries could not rely on the rhetorical persuasiveness or the assumed spiritual power of their message alone. They could not simply introduce a worldview and expect it to triumph by force of reason. The missionaries had rather to undermine the authority of the priestesses and age grade councillors, and to falsify (or at least render obsolete) traditional beliefs by demonstrating that good harvests and victory in war did not depend on them but could come via Dutch-prescribed channels of technical and spiritual power. To give force to their message, the Dutch had to create a new structure of authority that could command obedience and provide incentives for compliance.[7]

Notes

1. The presumption that Junius was marrying according to church rites (Campbell 1903:348) primarily young couples is supported by a 1644 report proposing civil marriages for older couples:

> As there are many aged heathen of both sexes who live together as husbands and wives, and who cannot easily be instructed in the Christian religion, it has been decided by the Consistory that each of those couples will be allowed to continue living under one roof, but on condition that they be united in marriage by the judicial functionary, this officer taking pains to impress upon them the signification of the marriage tie. [Campbell 1903:202]

A 1642 report explains that the missionaries were having greater success converting younger people:

> The younger people are regularly and easily instructed in the principles of our religion, as well as in the art of writing. We have greater difficulty with people who are more advanced in years. It seems they cannot abandon the nature of the first Adam, and that they still secretly retain their old superstitions. [Campbell 1903:189]

Although the missionaries regarded the young as eager learners and therefore more receptive to new doctrines, my analysis of the costs and benefits of the Sirayan system of marriage for the young and old suggests that the young also had considerably more to gain from the missionaries' injunction to establish conjugal households at an early age. Because the new doctrines meant an erosion of the status and powers of the old over the young, elders found the new teachings less attractive.

2. For a more detailed account and references, see Shepherd 1993.

3. To the Sinkandians the issue was less a matter of whether the Dutch god was true and their gods false, and more a question of compatibility among jealous, rival gods.

4. The Sirayan abandonment of abortion under new political circumstances is not unlike the ready abandonment of elaborate male initiation rituals by New Guinea groups following pacification (R. Keesing 1982:16, 37). These radical social transformations in which institutions (that some schools of anthropology identify as central to a group's ecological adaptation or processes of personality formation) are suddenly and completely abandoned raise serious questions about anthropological models of society that assume high degrees of cultural integration or that institutions primarily evolve as adaptations to economic environments, and support in their stead models that emphasize the political, conventional, and arbitrary nature of human culture and institutions.

5. For more discussion of the impact on Sirayan society of Dutch rule in Taiwan, see Shepherd 1993. The ready abandonment of abortion, once the political environment was transformed, further supports rejection of the arguments that mandatory abortion served to relieve the pressure of population on resources, or to maximize female labor for agriculture or deerskin processing. Concerns about overpopulation or a female labor shortage resulting from the abolition of abortion are never expressed in the Dutch records.

6. The change in timing of joint residence undoubtedly had an impact on the structure of the matrifocal household; in particular the earlier introduction

of inmarrying husbands would require adjustments in the relations between the young couple and the senior generation, who had previously had exclusive rights to the services of young adult daughters (and sons). Under the new regime, Siraya households became extended families containing parents, daughters, inmarrying husbands, and young children, on the model found among the Ami. There is no reason to suspect that the change in marriage practice led to virilocal marriages, for that would have upset the allocation of rights in land to matrifocal households, as well as the cooperation among sisters in agriculture and domestic management, and there are no reports hinting of such changes. Note that conjugal coresidence by young couples among the Ami was fully compatible with uxorilocal households and agriculture by matrifocal units (Liu 1965; Yuan 1969).

7. Once destroyed, the intellectual basis and structural props of mandatory abortion had no means of making a comeback—even after the Dutch had been expelled from Taiwan. At the very least, the processes of economic and ecological degradation experienced by the Siraya hunting economy meant that the primitive affluence that was necessary to mitigate the demographic consequences of mandatory abortion would never return.

8
Conclusions

The Sirayan system of delayed transfer uxorilocal marriage did not allow men to take up residence with their wives or to rear children until after they had completed service as warriors and hunters on behalf of their age grade and natal households.[1] The Siraya also expected husbands to reside uxorilocally and to rear their children jointly with their wives. The Siraya reconciled these two principles by requiring young wives to abort all pregnancies until their husbands completed their years of age grade service and took up residence uxorilocally. Thus the Sirayan system of kinship and marriage provides a temporal/sequential solution to the contest of loyalties posed by the "matrilineal puzzle": married men served their age grades and natal households in their youth, and retired from the age grade system to raise families uxorilocally only on reaching their forties. So long as marital and extramarital sex were enjoyed by the young, abortion by young wives was a necessary concomitant of the Sirayan marriage system. Indeed, a young married woman who did not abort but bore her child would be creating for her husband a conflict of loyalties between his duties to his age grade and natal household, on the one hand, and his duties to his wife and children, on the other; this was the very conflict that delayed transfer uxorilocal marriage in conjunction with mandatory abortion helped to avoid. These institutions drew their meaning from the complex of pregnancy taboos that warned of the spiritual danger of a wife's pregnancy to a husband's safe return from headhunting.

The Sirayan cultural system, in its social structural opposition of male age grade service and conjugal residence, its belief in the mystical incompatibility of headhunting and childbearing, and its mandatory practice of massage abortion, represents an extreme development of themes and techniques that we have found widespread in Formosan aboriginal and Austronesian cultures. What led to this extremity of development in the Sirayan case—perhaps intense warfare leading to severe age grade discipline, religious radicalism demanding abortion for headhunters' wives, or the war of the sexes and generations sharpening division between male and female spheres (all in the context of a primitive affluence and population structure capable of accommodating great delays in childbearing)—is a historical problem buried in a past that lies beyond our reach. But we have been able in this monograph to document and analyze the form taken by Sirayan culture and society and even to suggest some of the dynamic tensions creating this form, at the conjuncture reached in the early 17th century.

The complexity of social and cultural phenomena guarantees that no single interpretation or theoretical perspective will be capable of capturing all its dimensions. Productive insights come from recognizing both the possibility of a multiplicity of perspectives, and the need to subject each in its turn to critical scrutiny and evidentiary tests. Because some recent anthropology relies more on melodramatic rhetoric than intellectual rigor in reaching its conclusions (cf. Merquior 1985; Kapferer 1988), I wish to note some of the methodological approaches employed here to avoid the more obvious pitfalls awaiting social analysis. I have attempted in creating my own reconstruction of the nexus surrounding Sirayan mandatory abortion to locate it within the cultural and social structural context of early 17th-century Siraya history. I have tried to show the power of this reconstruction by its ability to account consistently and coherently for the wide range of features of Sirayan society reported in the historical record. I have drawn out the logical consequences of the reconstruction and sought to test these for their plausibility. I have tested parts of the reconstruction against modern bodies of knowledge: massage abortion against knowledge of female reproductive physiology, and the extended delay of childbearing caused by mandatory abortion against the learning of historical demography. I have also entertained alternative explanations—for example, population pressure, cultural materialism, Freudian psychodynamics (see Appendix A)—and marshalled arguments and evidence to test their plausibility. In the course of critiquing a series of functionalist explanations offered for Sirayan mandatory abortion, identifying the numerous functional alternatives to abortion has highlighted the need to account for the cultural and historical specificities of the Sirayan case. Controlled comparisons (especially with the closely related and similarly structured Ami and Puyuma) have further refined the analysis by narrowing its focus to features distinguishing the Siraya case (cf. Eggan 1954). I have also used the controlled comparison afforded by historical change to test the plausibility of the reconstruction against the means by which the Dutch missionaries undermined the institutions of mandatory abortion and delayed transfer uxorilocal marriage (cf. Fischer 1970).

Only by testing competing hypotheses against the evidence can anthropologists properly evaluate the merits of any analysis. The fashionable but mistaken contrast between "interpretation" and "explanation" disguises this point, and often operates as an attempt to evade critical scrutiny (cf. O'Meara 1989). Interpretations of cultural phenomena are no more than explanatory hypotheses, however they are labeled, and should not on any account be exempted from being tested against the evidence, and evaluated against alternative hypotheses. Multiple interpretations of the same phenomena are always possible, but they cannot all be equally valid and powerful. It is only through rigorous testing and critical examination that the strengths and weaknesses of plausible interpretations can emerge.

Note

1. Stockard (1989) documents a form of "delayed transfer" *virilocal* marriage among Cantonese Chinese, and I have adapted her term. In Stockard's case the delayed transfer refers to the delay in the transfer of a married woman to her husband's family. Many societies organize marriage as a process, spread over a long series of separate stages. Nuer brides, for instance, do not take up residence with their husbands until they have borne and weaned their first child (Evans-Pritchard 1951:72–73).

Appendix A: Freudian Perspectives

My review of the range of theoretical approaches that have been used to analyze the Sirayan case would not be complete without considering the Freudian interpretation of Sirayan abortion proposed by the ethnopsychiatrist George Devereux. Freudian theories purport to reveal the psychological conflicts underlying individual behavior and, more ambitiously, to account for configurations of culture and personality.

Devereux bases his interpretation of Siraya abortion on the Freudian theory of female penis envy. Freud asserted that, when young girls discover that boys have penises and girls do not, they develop penis envy. This discovery causes girls to turn away from attachment to their mothers, whom they blame for their lack of a penis, and to begin to prefer their fathers, who have the organ they lack. In Freudian theory, female penis envy is the counterpart of a boy's castration fear.[1] A maturing girl eventually "gives up her wish for a penis and puts in place of it a wish for a child," (Freud 1977:340). Thus Freud, and his follower Devereux, posit for women an unconscious psychic equation of penis = child (Freud 1977:340; Devereux 1976: 95, 146). After reviewing three clinical cases of women exhibiting a *"neurotic initial wish* to become pregnant, *so as to be able to abort,"* (1976:384, emphasis in original) Devereux concludes:

> Paradoxical as it may seem—for pregnancy and having a child usually tend to *compensate* woman for her "lack" of a penis—the desire to abort actually represents an unconscious attempt to *negate* that women are born "castrated."
>
> Indeed, since for most women an abortion represents castration, for women with a certain kind of personality make-up, the fact that they *can* abort (be "castrated") seems to constitute *prima facie* evidence that they were not *born* "castrated." [Devereux 1976:386, emphasis in original]

This follows because psychoanalytically penis = child and castration = abortion. Childbirth compensates for lack of a penis in "normal" women who have outgrown penis envy, while abortion demonstrates denial of the lack of a penis for some neurotic women. Devereux applies this Freudian logic to the Siraya case:

> Women who abort repeatedly (Cf . . . the Formosan data . . .), may well seek to assert by these means that, despite repeated "castrations" (abortions), they retain the capacity to "regenerate" the lost phallus (= child)—thus demonstrating that they are "uncastratable." In such instances the abortion is clearly a "triumphal" one—and this quite apart from the fact that, just like a murder, abortion, and especially recurrent abortion, gives the woman

the feeling that she is the (more or less magical) mistress of life and death—including her own. [Devereux 1976:386]

Under this theory, women motivated by unresolved penis envy demonstrate that they are uncastratable by repeatedly aborting their pregnancies. Devereux thus seeks to use psychoanalytic insights obtained from Western clinical cases to illuminate the Sirayan practice of abortion. This interpretive method was pioneered by Freud, who subtitled his *Totem and Taboo* as *Some Points of Agreement between the Mental Lives of Savages and Neurotics* (1950).[2]

Devereux's Freudian interpretation of Siraya abortion as "castration-negating triumphal abortion" (1976:387) is flawed by numerous logical and empirical problems. First is the analogy of Siraya women to neurotic women patients who desired to become pregnant solely in order to be able to abort. Are we to assume that all young Sirayan women were the victims of such neurotic desires? Devereux's psychoanalytic perspective assumes that the Sirayan practice of abortion is motivated by individual psychological conflicts. But Siraya women practiced abortion in response to a societal institution that *mandated* abortion, regardless of the inclinations of individual young women, and whether they harbored neurotic desires or not.[3]

Second, given Freud's universal assumptions about the feminine psychology of penis envy, why should Sirayan women, compared to women in all other cultures, abort so frequently? What is it about the Siraya that makes Freud's psychological assumptions yield such a peculiar (and "neurotic") result in the Sirayan case? By itself, Freudian theory is unable to explain why the Sirayans, alone of all the Formosan headhunters, mandated abortion.

Third, Devereux's Freudian theory is troubled by the problem of functional equivalents. If child = penis, would not infanticide rather than abortion provide a more dramatic demonstration of a woman's power to deny castration and to arbitrate life and death? And would not the safe delivery of a healthy child also demonstrate a triumph over castration and death, as among the Belu of Timor?[4] Why don't Sirayan women resolve their penis envy normally through multiple childbirth rather than neurotically through multiple abortions? Devereux leaves all these questions unanswered.

Fourth, what is the relation between the *institution* of mandatory abortion and the neurotic penis envy Devereux attributes to Sirayan women? Does mandatory abortion resolve psychological conflicts common to all Siraya women? In another passage Devereux provides this Freudian theory of social institutions:

> No basic and strong impulse, acted out in an undisguised and socially approved form, needs a high degree of institutionalization. Only attitudes and impulses which are reaction formations against, or sublimations of, the repressed opposite drives need such institutional crutches. [Devereux 1976:155–156]

Devereux offers this theory in his account of societies that paradoxically institutionalize premarital cohabitation and yet condemn any resulting pregnancies and require their abortion. These cases offer a close parallel to the Siraya, whose pre-transfer stage of marriage provides, like a stage of premarital cohabitation, an institutionalized sexual outlet, yet is not expected to result in the production of children. In these cases, Devereux finds at work an "anal Puritanism," rather than a neurotic penis envy. He argues that an "anal obsessive attempt to systematize" (1976:156) explains both the institutionalization of premarital cohabitation ("[s]ince sex could not be altogether stopped") and the Puritanical condemnation of unwanted premarital pregnancies. Thus, the "institutionalization of premarital cohabitation is, *per se*, an expression of a basic 'puritanism' rooted in anality, which finds a concentrated outlet in a 'paradoxical' condemnation of premarital pregnancy resulting from institutionalized premarital cohabitation" (Devereux 1976:157). Here we can draw from Devereux an alternative Freudian theory, one that is rooted in anal Puritanism and that could account for both the pretransfer stage of Siraya marriage and mandatory abortion. But the same objections hold for anal Puritanism as for neurotic penis envy: we still need an explanation why either pattern should be so excessively developed in the Siraya case.

A fifth problem is the plausibility of Freudian psychoanalytical theory itself. Is either Freudian hypothesis (female penis envy or anal Puritanism) necessary (or adequate) to account for abortion, whether that abortion be an individual choice, or in conformity to a social mandate? We could extend Devereux's Freudian interpretation to Siraya males: why not argue that headhunting is the male counterpart of female abortions? Successful headtaking surely marks for males a triumph over death, and since to Freudians, head = phallus, repeated headtakings must also demonstrate that a headhunter who "castrates" others is himself uncastratable. But why privilege female penis envy and male castration anxiety? A (non-Freudian) theory of male womb envy could provide equally plausible interpretations. Perhaps headhunters act out of male womb envy when they capture a trophy head and claim it is pregnant with seed and procreative power (head=womb, not phallus, cf. Bettelheim 1954:20).[5] The hypothesis of male womb envy also suggests that a rule of mandatory abortion may reflect male jealousy and aggression toward pregnant females rather than female penis envy.

These counterhypotheses challenge Freud's fundamental assumptions, but they suffer from the same problems (listed above) that all attempts to reduce sociocultural phenomena to private psychological conflicts must face. And neither womb envy, penis envy, nor anal Puritanism, is supported by specifically Siraya evidence.

Notes

1. In Freud's oedipal theory, a boy, in seeking exclusive possession of his mother, becomes jealous of his father as a rival for motherly affection. A boy's subsequent discovery that girls lack penises creates a fear of castration by the paternal rival. Castration anxiety then leads to repression or destruction of desire for the mother and hostility toward the father, and results in increasing identification with the father. This process of identification results in incorporation of paternal authority in a developing superego and has no counterpart in women (Freud 1977:341–342; Hall 1954:109–110).

2. In an extended defense of this methodology, Devereux asserts that cross-cultural phenomena "almost automatically fall into several categories which constitute the conceptual framework of psychoanalysis" (1976:71–73).

3. This is not to deny the possibility of personal expression within the context of these institutions; cf. Leach 1958 and Obeyesekere 1981.

4. Hoskins reports that the Belu of Timor analogize successful childbirth (*not* abortion) to headhunting: "When a new mother comes out of a month or two of seclusion following childbirth, she is dressed with the clothing and decorations of a male headhunter. The victory that she and her child have achieved over pain, and their surviving a potentially dangerous life-crisis, is celebrated as if it were a victory at war" (Hoskins 1988:54).

5. Freeman documents the "head = phallus" equation among Freudians in his interpretation of Iban headhunting (1979:236–237). Davison and Sutlive (1991) provide an extended ritual and symbolic analysis of the Iban linkage of fertility and headhunting that challenges Freeman's phallic interpretation. They show that the headhunting rituals operate on a metaphor of vegetative reproduction that analogizes the head to seed-bearing fruit (head = womb?) and infants (Davison and Sutlive 1991:203).

Appendix B: Uxorilocality, Endogamy, and Male Age Grades: An Organizational Nexus

The prominent role of the male age grade in Siraya and Ami society is a feature that demands explanation, and whose correlates should be explored. I turn in this appendix to review some comparative propositions that relate age grade organizations to other features of societies, primarily at the level of social morphology. Analysis of the Siraya and Ami cases suggests that in their social organization these societies achieved an unusual "fit" between male age grade organization and household structure based on uxorilocal marriage. This appears to be unusual, for in the comparative literature male age grade organizations are most commonly associated with patrilineal kinship, so much so that a recent survey concluded that "the correlation with matrilineal systems is virtually absent," (Bernardi 1985:14, 141).[1] From this perspective, the Siraya and Ami, and other societies with similar organizational features, constitute a set of deviant cases that should be brought to the attention of comparativists.

What follows is an abstract analysis contrasting certain consequences of uxorilocal and virilocal forms of marriage, consideration of some sociological hypotheses put forth in the cross-cultural literature, and a survey of some cases exhibiting features of social structure similar to the Siraya and Ami. The discussion is intended to raise questions about the comparative literatures that are suggested by our analysis of the Siraya. The focus is on the fit between age grades and uxorilocal household organization, hence the importance given to rules of post-marital residence rather than the reckoning of "kinship" along patrilineal or matrilineal lines.

We noted in our discussion of Sirayan demographics in Chapter 3 that Sirayan villages were markedly large concentrations of population, averaging 1000 but ranging as high as 3000. This is part of a more general contrast among Formosan aboriginal groups between (1) large, endogamous villages of matrilocally organized households with age sets and men's houses (Siraya, Ami, Puyuma) and (2) small, exogamous villages of patrilocally organized households (Bunun, Atayal) (Shepherd 1993:38–46; Mabuchi 1960). The explanation offered for the large average village size was derived from a structural consequence of uxorilocal marriage and matrilineal kinship. Married men seek to minimize the distance between the two groups that divide their loyalties: their own natal groups where they retain membership and exercise some authority, and the groups where their wives and children reside. This can be accomplished by marrying within the village, and village endogamy is a common solution to this problem (Gough 1961:559–561; Schneider 1961:27; Fox 1967:101–103). But a rule of village endogamy creates an additional problem, for if the incest taboo puts many village women in an unmarriageable category, men will be unable to find an eligible mate unless the village has a sizeable population. Thus village settlements in societies where men marry uxorilocally are often observed to contain large numbers of unrelated households.[2]

A village society so constituted faces the problem of structuring relations among its many households. This is usually a problem of structuring relations among the males who dominate the extradomestic sphere, rule over the village politically, manage intervillage relations, and exercise divided authority within its constituent households.[3] This problem exists for relations among households (and males) related through kinship and marriage, as well as for relations among households (and males) unrelated by either kinship or marriage.

There are important disruptions in the relations among males in matrilineal societies that practice uxorilocal residence: a boy is socialized with his brothers under the authority of their father, but at marriage leaves these male relationships to take up residence in his wife's household where authority is exercised by males previously unrelated to him. There, as an inmarrying husband, he will be subject to his wife's father and mother's brothers and come into contact with her brothers and her sisters' husbands, and his own sons will leave on marriage to be replaced by his daughters' husbands. As an adult male he will continue to exercise some authority in his natal household, where he will come into contact with his sisters' husbands, sons, daughters, and daughters' husbands. Thus each household will be caught in a web of conflicting male authority relations deriving from the dual role that each male plays as husband in his wife's household and brother in his natal household. This dual role results from the importance to males of both natal ties, which determine group membership and succession in matrilineal societies, and conjugal ties, which determine the male's relationship to his wife and children, who are members of a separate group (see Figure 2).[4]

This discontinuity in male relations and the dispersal of male authority between two households in a uxorilocal marriage system contrasts with the continuity and concentration possible in viri-patrilocal systems. Where men bring wives to reside with them in their natal group, the intermale relations that they grew up in, those with the father and brothers, will be the same relations that structure the relations between their separate households after marriage. And the relations a man and his wife develop with their own sons will structure the relations between their household and that of their sons after the sons marry. In the viri-patrilocal system, male-male relations (between brothers, fathers, and sons) are continuous throughout the male life-span and provide a grid for the structuring of relations among the spatially concentrated households of male kin, where each male's authority is discretely exercised (without interference from the wife's brother). Thus the (patrilineal) kinship of males structures the relations of households in a way that is not possible for systems practicing uxori-matrilocal marriage.[5] Indeed, small groups of patrilineally related households can form independent, spatially isolated, and exogamous villages, related to other such units by weak affinal relations created through the exchange of women. Societies constituted in this way need not create a non-kin-based villagewide system of male relations uniting disparate households, for patrilineal kinship already structures male and interhousehold relations, and there is no need (arising from the structure of kinship, at least) to concentrate unrelated or affinally related households in the same village.

But this patrilocal/patriarchal solution is not available to societies practicing uxorilocal marriage in the context of large endogamous villages. These societies must create non-kin-based structures of male and household interrelations to order the relations of males from unrelated and affinally related households and contain the potentially tense relations between males related through marriage. These relations may be strained because inmarrying husbands must compete with fathers-in-law and brothers-in-law to exercise authority over the same uterine families (a mother and her children).[6] This contrasts with virilocal marriage, where the spouse marrying into the family is a young wife who initially, at least, lacks authority (in the virilocal case it is the relations of females that are made discontinuous).[7]

Thus societies practicing uxorilocal marriage in the context of large endogamous villages may use age grades or other villagewide institutions to structure the relations of males and households. Systems of graded male age sets can create a continuous set of hierarchical relationships between males that cover their entire life-span and can establish a corporate entity with clear lines of authority, both aspects of intermale relations missing from systems of matrifocal households and uxorilocal marriage. In this sense male age grades in the context of uxorilocal households may be seen to operate as the functional equivalents of patrilineages in the context of virilocal households.

The importance of male communal institutions in matrifocal/matrilineal systems derives from the consequences of a definition of the adult male role as dual, divided between husband and brother roles, where each male retains important ties with both his natal and his conjugal unit. The organization of these units prevents his uniting them in the way accomplished in patrilineal systems, where the bride is removed from her natal group and relocated in her husband's natal group, where she will reproduce his group. Even in the viri-avunculocal solution that removes the wife from her natal group, there is still a discontinuity in male relations caused by the removal, at or before marriage, of the son from his father's group to his maternal uncle's group. In all the matrilineal cases, the father's domestic group is necessarily divided from his adult son's domestic group. This may be because it is his sister who reproduces his group, not his wife, and he will be succeeded by his nephew, not his son, as in the avunculocal solution (cf. Fox 1967:120–121) or because he sends his sons to marry elsewhere and keeps his daughters in his household in the uxorilocal solution.[8]

Several of the distinctive features of matrilineal descent groups delineated by Schneider (1961) imply connections among uxorilocal marriage, village endogamy, large village size, and male communal institutions. Schneider noted matrilineal groups face special problems, first in the organization of inmarrying males within households, especially in the relations between fathers-in-law and sons-in-law, but also among brothers-in-law (1961:20–21). Second, the spatial separation of conjugal and natal households poses problems for the fulfillment of the dual husband/brother role (1961:27). Schneider also noted that demographic vagaries frequently make it impossible to divide matrifocal households by pairing brothers to reproductive sisters in independent segments (1961:26–27). This makes it difficult for matrilineal systems to produce descent groups with internally ranked segments which can organize large populations. This problem arises because matrilineal kinship divides points of group segmentation (sisters and offspring) from the foci of group authority (brothers), and creates the problem of pairing the two points in independent segments. (Not only may the number of sisters not match the number of brothers, but a principle would be needed to allocate sisters among brothers.) Many problems of discontinuity and unclear ranking result. Mary Douglas adds to this point by noting that large, genealogically articulated lineages are rare in matrilineal systems in part because the fertility of any particular woman is limited, while polygyny allows at least some men in patrilineal systems to produce large numbers of heirs (1969:125). Douglas also notes that, because they lack principles ranking male members ("fraternal succession in a wide range of collateral lines makes for confusion in the second generation," 1969:129), matrilineal groups have problems allocating authority among males. Thus matrilineal kinship regularly fails to provide clear lines of authority both between and within domestic segments.

In patrilineal systems, men (each matched with wives) are the points both of segmentation and authority; thus the grid of male authority relations simultaneously maps the relations of segments. In matrilineal societies, concentrating both conjugal and natal households in the same village solves the spatial problem for males serving in divided roles but creates the problem of how male and household interrelations are to be organized. Male communal institutions such as age grades are common solutions to these political problems, for they provide a non-kin-based structure of authority for males and households brought together by village endogamy and divided male roles. This is the organizational nexus of uxorilocality, endogamy, and male age grades that the Siraya and Ami cases illustrate.

Cross-cultural research on warfare and age-sets has produced a number of hypotheses that relate aspects of the organizational nexus of uxorilocality and endogamy to processes of social conflict. These hypotheses point to new sets of interrelations that deserve our consideration.[9] Ember and Ember found that, in contrast to patrilocal (virilocal) societies, matrilocal (uxorilocal) societies were less likely to engage in warfare between neighboring and intermarrying communities and more likely to engage only in "external" warfare against other societies (Ember and Ember 1971: 582–583). Noting that patrilocality dispersed the women of a group and that matrilocality dispersed the men, they reasoned that:

> fighting between such intermarrying (probably neighboring) communities should not be as likely in matrilocal as in patrilocal societies. This is because if warfare between intermarrying communities were to occur, the men who are living in other than their natal communities would have to participate in the initiation of warfare against the very communities in which they and their wives and children reside. Such a conflict between a man's community of orientation and his community of procreation cannot occur in patrilocal societies, and hence (functionally speaking) fighting between neighboring or intermarrying communities should occur more often in patrilocal than in matrilocal societies. [Ember and Ember 1971:582]

Because men have ties stretching between two communities in a system of uxorilocal residence, the Embers predict their divided loyalties will impede the escalation of intercommunity conflict. By contrast, in a virilocal system it is women rather than men whose ties stretch between two communities, but their divided loyalties will have less effect in dampening conflict because women are rarely given voice in decisions regarding war and peace. In their hypothetical case, Ember and Ember have assumed that the men in a uxorilocal system will marry into nearby villages rather than endogamously (they do note that very few matrilineal societies mandate local exogamy) (1971:581). Whether the intermarrying unit is the large endogamous village or a group of neighboring small villages should make little difference; in both cases the divided loyalties of the men should mean that conflict will be muted within the intermarrying unit and any warfare directed outside it.

We may also view the uxorilocal system as one in which a senior male can create a wide network of ties through his outmarrying sons as well as his inmarrying sons-in-law, all of whom retain relations with both their natal and conjugal families and communities. By contrast a senior male in a patrilocal system will have a weaker network of affinal relations based on the exchange of women, who play a much less significant role in war and peacemaking, but he will have his closest male relations (his brothers and sons) concentrated around him. Mary Douglas emphasizes the positive advantage of matriliny where intergroup alliance is strong and group-exclusiveness weak: "Where intermarriage takes the form of exchange of males, the cross-cutting ties which make for a criss-cross of reciprocal obligations are carried by the dominant sex. This implies more emphasis on intergroup alliance than in a system where the cross-cutting ties are carried by the weaker sex" (1969:126). Thus if "alliance" and peacekeeping were the goal of marriage exchanges, it should be males and not females who are exchanged, contra Lévi-Strauss 1969:68.

Divale (1984) has replicated Ember and Ember's findings of an association between matrilocal residence and external war, and related this finding to "fraternal interest group theory" and patterns of internal feuding. Previous studies have found a positive association between the localization of agnatically related males through patrilocal residence and the presence of feuding within a society (Divale 1984:15–18).[10] Divale goes on to argue that matrilocal organization, because it disperses fraternal interest groups, reduces internal feuding, and thereby makes large-scale united action possible, will have a selective advantage over patrilocal organization when a society is threatened by external warfare (1984:21–26).[11] Divale, like the Embers, assumes that most matrilocal societies disperse their outmarrying males beyond the local community and that such spatial dispersal is crucial to reducing the feuding that arises when fraternal interest groups are localized (1984:21).[12]

Divale thus ignores the many instances of matrilocal societies, such as the Siraya and Ami of Taiwan, whose villages are endogamous. Indeed, Murdock found "a nearly universal association between matrilocal residence in sedentary communities and local endogamy" (Murdock 1949:214; see also Kloos 1963). Many of these endogamous and uxorilocal societies have developed institutions, like age sets, that order the relations of the males in the community on a non-kin basis and create bonds that cross-cut fraternal groups.

Cross-cultural research on age-sets has shown that where they occur, age-sets are almost always associated with frequent warfare (Ritter 1980:94–96).[13] Hanson has pointed out some of the organizational requirements of supporting an age-set system in which homogeneous age-groups pass through a sequence of grades:

> In order for the age-set structure to perpetuate itself, a relatively continuous supply of eligible cohorts is necessary. . . . [T]o achieve this, local groups . . . must maintain a high degree of demographic and territorial stability. They must . . . maintain a local population large enough to produce viable age cohorts so that the layering of military groups by age is feasible. [J. Hanson 1988:357]

One place the concentrated populations necessary to support age-set systems will be found is in large, endogamous villages united by the threat of frequent external war. If the households in these villages are matrilocally organized, the resulting dispersal of fraternal groups may reduce levels of internal feuding and make it easier to enforce the discipline of the age-set system. These considerations point again to the organizational linkage of uxorilocality, endogamy, and male age grades.

In North America, age-sets are found among only five northern Plains groups and are believed to have originated among two of these groups, the Mandan and the Hidatsa. Both the Mandan and the Hidatsa were matrilineal, matrilocal groups that lived in large, locally en- dogamous, fortified villages and engaged in frequent warfare. Hanson sees Mandan age-set organization as developing after the Mandan changed their settlement pattern from dispersed, small villages to dense, fortified villages in response to conflict with encroaching Arikara groups to the immediate south (J. Hanson 1988:359). Once the model of age-set organization was developed and had proved its value, it spread to neighboring Arapahoe, Gros Ventre and Blackfoot groups, where it cross-cut kin groups and integrated bands (J. Hanson 1988:361).[14]

Several studies of Amazon groups have noted a contrast between the large villages of the Ge and Bororo on the central plateau and the much smaller villages in the forested river basins (Gross 1979:325–326; Turner 1979a:174–175; Shapiro 1987:304). In social structural terms this appears to parallel the difference between large, endogamous villages of matrilocally organized households with age sets and men's houses (Siraya, Ami, Puyuma) and small, exogamous villages of patrilocally organized households (Bunun, Atayal) noted for aboriginal Taiwan

(Shepherd 1993:38–46; Mabuchi 1960). The ability of the various Ge groups to form large nucleated settlements that make heavy subsistence demands on the surrounding area has also been related to the richness of the environment they occupy and the diversity of their techniques for exploiting both the hunting and horticultural opportunities it provides (Gross 1979:328–329; Turner 1979a:148–149, 175–176). But we must still ask why the Ge congregate in large villages, for a generous environment does not require that the populations it supports live in dense, nucleated settlements. Turner and Gross offer competing explanations.

Turner's answer to why the Ge have communal organizations and large village size is rooted in his answer to why they practice uxorilocal marriage. Turner sees the Ge and Bororo political economies as based on the exploitation of young men and women by older men; because older men can more easily control daughters than sons, older men gain leverage over younger men (sons-in-law) through the uxorilocal marriages of their daughters (1979a:158–159, 168). In Turner's view male communal organization is necessary to ensure the dominance of senior males over juniors and to structure the exchange of sons and sons-in-law between households headed by fathers and fathers-in-law (1979a:166–167). The existence of communal institutions enables these villages to integrate large numbers of households; this in turn produces large, endogamous villages (1979a:174). Turner's model and the central role in it of exploitative intergenerational relations seems based on the specifics of the Kayapo case, which is extreme in severing a young man's relations with his natal group and subordinating him to his father-in-law (Turner 1979b:181), although Turner allows that, as the son-in-law's own family of procreation matures, his relations with his parents-in-law are characterized more and more not by dominance but by reciprocity (1979b:187). Other Ge societies have quite positive and cooperative relations between fathers and sons (Maybury-Lewis 1979a:234). This subverts the (oedipal) assumption implicit in Turner's model that uxorilocality is necessary because, while fathers may control daughters, cooperative father-son relations (and therefore virilocality) cannot obtain (1979a:158–159). An alternative view would see sons choosing uxorilocal residence because of the inability of fathers to provide wives for their sons.[15]

But if Turner's model is overly specific, and fails to accommodate the other Ge and Bororo societies (Maybury-Lewis 1979b:304), an alternative model proposed by Maybury-Lewis that emphasizes male-female dualism (1979a:234) is too general. The symbolic contrast between a male public sphere and a female domestic sphere is found in a great many societies (many of which are organized patrilineally and do not divide adult males between conjugal and natal ties, brother and husband roles). Nor can male-female dualism account for uxorilocality, for women organized virilocally (mothers and their sons' wives) may also be restricted to a female domestic sphere.

Gross relates large village size among the Ge to warfare conducted in the context of a particular pattern of agriculture:

> Elsewhere in lowland South America, warfare and the threat of attack favor the dispersal of groups into small villages. . . . But this option was not open to Central Brazilians since suitable garden land was available only along the highly exposed river banks. Thus large villages were formed as defense or deterrence against armed attacks. [1979:331]

Forced by the vulnerable location of their gardens to congregate in dense settlements, the Central Brazilians had then to find means of integrating the many unrelated households in their villages. Age sets and other male communal institutions that cut across kinship bonds and organized the males for war were the nearly universal solution (Gross 1979:334–335). While Gross notes that Ember and Ember (1971) had pointed out that uxorilocal residence by breaking up fraternal groups facilitated village integration, uxorilocal residence plays a very minor role in his model (1979:334). But it is possible that uxorilocal organization (and the networks of male alliances it creates), as much as the vulnerable location of gardens,[16] encouraged the Central Brazilians to defend themselves by congregating in large settlements, while virilocal organization and the formation of fraternal interest groups encouraged other lowland Amazonians to disperse themselves in small exogamous villages.[17]

One of the links between uxorilocality and male communal institutions is to be found in the strains uxorilocality puts on male roles of authority: it puts together in the same domestic unit a father-in-law (or brother-in-law) and a son-in-law who are strangers to one another prior to the marriage, it deprives any given male of exclusive authority over a domestic group by giving him the dual role of husband and brother and divided authority over his own wife and children and over his sisters and their children, it puts each uterine family between two competing males, and it requires that affinally related households and unrelated households be concentrated in the same village if the men are to be able to find wives and perform both their roles within the village. Male communal institutions serve to mediate these conflicts and strains in the relations between males and the households to which they are attached and the Ge and Bororo material gives plenty of evidence of just such strains (Maybury-Lewis 1979a:234; Crocker 1979:298–299).[18]

Africa does not appear to provide examples of endogamous communities of uxorilocal households united by age-grade systems; although matrilineal kinship and age grades are both commonly found there, they do not coincide. African matrilineal groups are overwhelmingly viri-avunculocal, often localized in exogamous avuncular clan communities (cf. Murdock 1959:84–85, 96, 99, 299; A. Schlegel 1972:53–54). The relations among males in such communities are structured by matrilineal kinship. In those parts of the matrilineal belt of Central Africa where uxorilocal residence is practiced, so is shifting cultivation; population is sparsely distributed, and large settlements do not occur (Richards 1950:247).

Age-grade systems are widespread in East Africa especially, but these serve primarily to unite communities of pastoral groups that are patrilocal and polygynous and that require substantial bridewealth for marriage (Murdock 1959:201–203, 326–327, 337–338), suggesting the age grades also serve to ensure senior male dominance over young men whose marriages are delayed. Age grades also occur in large dense settlements as among the Yoruba chieftaincies, where they cross-cut membership in patrilineages (Lloyd 1965:563). Among the matrilineal Ashanti who live in large dense settlements, postmarital residence is duolocal, interrupted by a period of virilocality when the children of the marriage are growing (Fortes 1970; Murdock 1959:256). Horton emphasizes the role in Ashanti chiefdoms of the young men's companies (stratified by age) that cut across matrilineage ties and unite the men of the settlement (Horton 1983:65–67). In these latter two cases, the unity of the settlement is achieved through centralized political institutions, rather than the age-set system.

This broad ranging comparative review suggests some of the sociological factors that make the co-occurrence of large village endogamy, age grades, uxorilocal marriage, and matrifocal households, as found among the Ami and the Siraya, a pattern common to a subset of cultures. I have not tried to explain the adoption of uxorilocality, endogamy, age-sets, or adult male roles divided between the roles of husband and brother. Instead, I have compared groups from Taiwan, the northern Plains, and lowland Amazonia to point up some striking similarities in the organizational patterns they have adopted and to suggest systemic interrelationships that account for the frequent co-occurence of uxorilocality, the division of adult male roles between husband and brother, large endogamous villages and male communal institutions. Taken separately these institutional patterns may be the result of any number of ideological constructions of gender, sexual divisions of labor, patterns of warfare, or ecological pressures. Detailed historical work (or at least controlled comparisons among closely related groups) will be needed to see if such comparative hypotheses can yield productive insights in the analysis of specific cases.[19]

Notes

1. Those who note the correlation of male age class systems with patrilineal structures commonly see one function of the age grades as reinforcing the authority of senior males over juniors. This is especially evident in bridewealth societies where the polygyny of senior males is achieved at the expense of a long delay in the marriages of junior males.

2. For an extended discussion of the puzzle of village size among aboriginal groups in Taiwan, see Shepherd 1993:38–46. Rather than start the analysis with matrifocal households, we could start with age grades. The independent development of strong age grade organization could lead to the requirement that men become permanent lifetime members of the age grade; in such a case postmarital residence must leave the men in place. If postmarital residence is uxorilocal, then men must marry endogamously if they are to remain permanently in the village and the age grade. If postmarital residence is viri-patrilocal, however, the rule of endogamy may be relaxed, because the residence of men is undisturbed by marriages in which wives move in and sisters move out.

3. Some descriptions of Minangkabau villages suggest male authority was very limited even in the extradomestic sphere (Peletz 1987:453).

4. Cross-cousin marriage, though rarely statistically significant, is a frequently discussed solution to the problem of discontinuity in male relations in uxorilocal households. Matrilateral cross-cousin marriage enables a man to bring his sister's son into his wife's household as his daughter's husband. Patrilateral cross-cousin marriage enables a man to place his own son in his sister's household as his sister's daughter's husband (A. Schlegel 1972:10–12, 107–121). Cross-cousin marriage thus can be used to place a kinsman in a role that would otherwise be filled by a stranger.

5. It is uxori-matrilocal (and duolocal) marriage that prevents the kinship of males from structuring household interrelations, not matrilineality per se, for where the postmarital residence rule is viri-avunculocal (common in Africa), the matrilineal kinship of mother's brother and sister's son will structure the relations between locally concentrated households. In a viri-avunculocal system, the sister's son, commonly at puberty or marriage, takes up residence near his mother's brother (e.g. on his uncle's land, which he expects to inherit matrilineally) and brings in a wife. The viri-avunculocal system still suffers from considerable discontinuity in the relations of males, who are socialized by their fathers but create their households near their maternal uncles and see their own sons leave to be replaced by nephews. Duolocal marriage systems more closely resemble uxorilocal marriage in that the dual role of the male as husband/brother is salient, with the balance tipped toward the brother role in the natal group.

6. The consequences of the dual role of the male as brother and husband in a matrilineal system may be looked at from another perspective: not only may male groups be necessary to contain the conflict created between men seeking to aggrandize power by dominating the households of both wives and sisters, male groups may be necessary as refuges for men whose wives and sisters compete to dominate them. Thus Crocker in discussing the Bororo comments:

> It is little wonder that the men, caught between the demands of their sisters and of their wives, choose to spend most of their time in the transitional

"middle ground" of the men's house, which is categorically forbidden to all women. [Crocker 1979:280]

7. There is no reason, of course, to assume in the viri-patrilocal case that relations among brothers are always harmonious or that the process of incorporating a stranger-wife is an easy one. Wives in these systems may be expected to challenge informally the structure of male relations, and their own domination by their mothers-in-law; cf. M. Wolf 1972 and A. Wolf 1986.

8. The duality of the male role may be seen to proceed from the definition of the reproductive capacity of women, for in a matrilineal society a woman reproduces her natal group (the group she shares with her brother) and not the group of her husband. Thus a man's children never belong to his group while his sister's children do. The woman is thus in a position to make demands of both her brother and her husband, and to play them off one against the other if she chooses.

9. I find cross-cultural research valuable not because its methodology of statistical correlation can "prove" its propositions (deviant cases, like the Siraya, are often the most interesting), but as an hypothesis-generating exercise. Wide-ranging comparisons on many dimensions are indispensable to overcoming the myopic pitfalls of individual ethnographies. Once hypotheses are generated, they are best evaluated with closely controlled comparisons and against the specifics of particular historical cases.

10. These studies also find a positive relationship between polygyny, patrilocal residence, and frequent feuding, suggesting that fraternal interest groups are fighting for access to women whose availability polygyny has reduced (Divale 1984:15–18). Thus the comparative absence of polygyny in uxorilocal (but not all matrilineal) societies must also contribute to their internal peacefulness, but Divale did not test for this relationship.

11. Postulating that this selective advantage was greatest when groups came into conflict during migrations, Divale develops a migration theory of the origin of matrilocality (1984:21–26). Migration, however, is only one possible circumstance that could cause external warfare and the postulated selective advantage to operate. In addition, Divale wavers as to whether both the migrating and the invaded indigenous society will develop matrilocality (1984:11, 22, 25, 51).

Divale postulates that a patrilocally organized group would adopt uxorilocality to offset the loss of males in warfare; this would result from fathers using the marriages of their daughters to recruit inmarrying sons-in-law. The resulting decline in feuding due to the dispersal of fraternal interest groups would confer a selective advantage, causing uxorilocality to spread as well through a demonstration effect (1984:23–24). This hypothesized scenario fails to answer why fathers would allow their own sons to marry out, thereby creating a truly uxorilocal system. It is possible that conditions of external warfare may have rewarded fathers who sought to create alliances between groups through a male network by sending out sons in marriage and recruiting inmarrying sons-in-law. These groups could remain dispersed or concentrate for purposes of defense. In contrast to Divale's migration-external war theory, Murphy gives an economic argument for a shift to uxorilocality. Murphy theorizes that the Mundurucu shifted from patrilocality to matrilocality with the external imposition of general peace and the growth of trade in manioc flour produced by women's groups. As this put a premium on the continuity of women's producer groups, a groom's bride-service was no longer considered to give him the right to remove his bride from her natal village and matrilocality became the rule (Murphy 1960:79–82, 181–183).

12. The locus classicus for this paradigm is Murphy's work on the Mundurucu (1960). The Mundurucu combined matrilocality with a high degree of male exogamy, a pattern that Murphy considered unusual. Outsider husbands were integrated into the village through residence in the village men's house, where they escaped domination by their fathers-in-law (1960:102–106). Adult males maintained relations with their natal groups, and war-parties were recruited through male networks from a number of villages (1960:127–128).

13. Ritter postulated that age-sets would be found in "frequently warring societies where the size and composition of the local group fluctuates throughout the year," reasoning that where descent groups dispersed and recongregated during the annual subsistence cycle an additional principle of organization would be needed to organize warfare by the entire group (1980:98). But because warfare is far more widespread than age sets, age-sets cannot be predicted by the presence of warfare. Hanson thus rejects Ritter's hypothesis for North America, where nearly all Plains groups had both warfare and seasonally fluctuating groups, but only a few had age-sets (J. Hanson 1988:354).

14. The Western Pueblos offer another North American example of dense, largely endogamous villages of matrilocally organized households. In these cases, not age grades, but ritual societies cut across clans and households to unite the village in a common ceremonial cycle (Eggan 1950:120; cf. Allen 1981).

15. Collier's comparative analysis and modeling of brideservice societies (1988:19) suggests that men leave the households of their fathers for those of their fathers-in-law not because of friction or intergenerational exploitation, but because the absence of strong senior generational authority over juniors (that in bridewealth societies enables an ordered exchange of women for valuables) means that fathers in bride service societies have no ability to get wives for their sons. Young males perform brideservice and take up uxorilocal residence because they look to the influence (not authority) of the wife's parents over their daughter to help preserve the marriage (and discourage lovers). Riviere also questions this aspect of Turner's model (Riviere 1984:96–98, 103ff.); he argues that the disadvantage of virilocality for Amazonians lies not in the troubled father-son relations emphasized by Turner but in the problem of organizing a balanced exchange of women between virilocal units: "for when control over a woman is surrendered there is no mechanism that assures replacement" (1984:105). In uxorilocal and endogamous villages, women and men marry without either spouse leaving the natal group's control. Meillassoux's (1981:28–31) evolutionary progression from gynecostatic to patrilineal organization completely misses the possibility of village endogamy, villages that are simultaneously "gynecostatic" and "phallostatic." Relevant here to a further critique of Meillassoux is the critique in Chapter 3 of Divale and Harris's model relating population and warfare.

16. It is beyond my competence to evaluate Gross's theory regarding the vulnerability of garden site locations. But in the search for patterns that explain why groups as diverse as the Ami and Siraya of Taiwan, the Mandan and Hidatsa of North America, and the Ge and Bororo of Central Brazil share certain organizational characteristics, particular ecological factors are unlikely to offer generalizeable hypotheses. Gross's paper is somewhat confusing as to whether he includes the Mundurucu, a non-Ge group, within his model. It seems clear that the Mundurucu do not fit the model, as (1) their savannah villages, where

they practiced horticulture, were located several hours from navigable streams (Murphy 1960:56), and (2) while practicing matrilocality, Mundurucu villages were predominantly exogamous for males and generally small (Murphy 1960:8, 85, 102).

17. Present-day Ge villages are often much smaller than they were in the past (Gross 1979:326, Turner 1979a:149–150) due in part to frequent fissioning and sharp division among factions (cf. Bamberger 1979:131–133). This appears to be due to the decline of age set institutions and a concomitant decline in village wide integration and the ability to suppress factional schisms (Maybury-Lewis 1967:301, 1979a:235–236; Lave 1979:36–44).

18. Maybury-Lewis has suggested the same strains in the male role leads to aggressiveness among Ge males and contributes to factionalism (1967:308–309), while I would emphasize that these strains, by alienating males from households and kin, make it easier for the age set system to achieve its integrative role. It is likely that the decline of external warfare has weakened the age-set systems and enabled factionalism to worsen among the Ge.

19. This comparative discussion suggests a number of hypotheses for future research: for example, holding ecological and warfare factors constant, will matrilocally organized groups form dense settlements integrated by male communal institutions more easily than patrilocally organized ones? Conversely, does it require a greater degree of outside pressure or political centralization and stratification for patrilocally organized groups to form dense settlements (where competition among fraternal interest groups could be expected to be intense) compared to matrilocally organized groups?

References Cited

Adelaar, Sander
 1994 Grammar Notes on Siraya, an Extinct Formosan Language. Paper presented at the Seventh International Conference of Austronesian Linguistics, August, Leiden, Netherlands.
Allen, Michael
 1981 Rethinking Old Problems: Matriliny, Secret Societies, and Political Evolution. *In* Vanuatu: Politics, Economics, and Ritual in Island Melanesia. Michael Allen, ed. Pp. 9–34. New York: Academic Press.
Atkinson, Jane
 1990 How Gender Makes a Difference in Wana Society. *In* Power & Difference: Gender in Island Southeast Asia. Jane M. Atkinson and S. Errington, eds. Pp. 59–93. Stanford, CA: Stanford University Press.
Bamberger, Joan
 1979 Exit and Voice in Central Brazil: The Politics of Flight in Kayapo Society. *In* Dialectical Societies: The Ge and Bororo of Central Brazil. David Maybury-Lewis, ed. Pp. 130–46. Cambridge, MA: Harvard University Press.
Barth, Fredrik
 1987 Cosmologies in the Making. Cambridge, England: Cambridge University Press.
Barton, Roy F.
 1938 Philippine Pagans: The Autobiographies of Three Ifugaos. London: George Rutledge & Sons.
Baudhuin, R. F., trans.
 1960 Selected Readings Translated from "Traditions and Myths of the Taiwan Aborigines" compiled by Ogawa and Asai. Manuscript in Fu Ssu-nien Library, Academia Sinica, Nankang, Taiwan.
Benedek, Dezso
 1987 A Comparative Study of the Bashiic Cultures of Irala, Ivatan, and Itbayat. Ph.D. dissertation, Pennsylvania State University.
Bernardi, Bernardo
 1985 Age Class Systems: Social Institutions and Polities Based on Age. Cambridge, England: Cambridge University Press.
Bettelheim, Bruno
 1954 Symbolic Wounds: Puberty Rites and the Envious Male. Glencoe, IL: Free Press.
Billig, Michael S.
 1992 The Marriage Squeeze and the Rise of Groomprice in India's Kerala State. Journal of Comparative Family Studies 23(2):197–216.
Bischofberger, Otto
 1972 Die Dienstwerbung des Madchens vor der Heirat bei den matrilinearen Amis (Taiwan). Anthropos 67:209–219.
 1976 Heil und Unheil, Gebete und Riten der Amis von Formosa. Freiburg, Switzerland: Universitatsverlag Freiburg Schweiz.
Blair, Emma H., and J. A. Robertson, eds.
 1903 The Philippine Islands, 1493–1803, Volume 7. Cleveland: A. H. Clark.

Bloch, Maurice, and J. Parry, eds.
    1982 Death and the Regeneration of Life. Cambridge, England: Cambridge
    University Press.
Blusse, Leonard
    1984 Dutch Protestant Missionaries as Protagonists of the Territorial Expan-
    sion of the VOC on Formosa. *In* Conversion, Competition, and Conflict:
    Essays on the Role of Religion in Asia. Dick Kooiman, Otto Vanden Mui-
    jzenberg, and Peter Van der Veer, eds. Pp. 155–184. Amsterdam: Free
    University Press.
Blusse, Leonard, and Marius Roessingh
    1984 A Visit to the Past: Soulang, A Formosan Village Anno 1623. Archipel
    27:63–80.
Borneo Literature Bureau
    1963 The Sea Dayaks and Other Races of Sarawak: Contributions to the
    Sarawak Gazette between 1888 and 1930. Hong Kong: South China Morning
    Post.
Buckley, Thomas, and Alma Gottlieb, eds.
    1988 Blood Magic: The Anthropology of Menstruation. Berkeley: University
    of California Press.
Campbell, William
    1903 Formosa under the Dutch; Described from Contemporary Records.
    London: Kegan Paul, Trench, Trubner & Co. Ltd. Reprint, 1967, Taipei:
    Ch'eng-wen.
Caso, Alfonso
    1958 The Aztecs: People of the Sun. Norman: University of Oklahoma Press.
Chai Chen-kang
    1967 Taiwan Aborigines: A Genetic Study of Tribal Variations. Cambridge,
    MA: Harvard University Press.
Chang Yao-ch'i
    1951 P'ing-p'u tsu she ming tui chao piao [A Comparative Namelist of
    P'ing-p'u Villages]. Wen-hsien chuan-k'an 2(1–2):insert.
Ch'en Chi-lu
    1965 Age Organization and Men's House of the Formosan Aborigines. Bul-
    letin of the Department of Archaeology and Anthropology [National Tai-
    wan University] 25–26:93–111.
    1968 The Material Culture of the Formosan Aborigines. Taipei: Taiwan
    Museum.
Ch'en Shih-chi
    1982 Student Teams Excavate 3000-year-old Tombs. Free China Review
    32(11) (November):35–37.
Ch'en Wen-te
    1986 A-mei tsu ch'in shu chih tu ti tsai t'an t'ao [Reconsideration of the Amis
    Kinship System]. Bulletin of the Institute of Ethnology, Academia Sinica
    61:41–80.
Coale, Ansley
    1974 The History of the Human Population. Scientific American 231(3):41–
    51.
Cohen, Mark N.
    1989 Health and the Rise of Civilization. New Haven, CT: Yale University
    Press.

Cole, Fay-Cooper
1913 The Wild Tribes of Davao District, Mindanao. Field Museum of Natural History Anthropological Series, 12.2. Chicago: Field Museum of Natural History.
1922 The Tinguian. Field Museum of Natural History Anthropological Series, 14.2. Chicago: Field Museum of Natural History.
Collier, Jane
1988 Marriage and Inequality in Classless Societies. Stanford, CA: Stanford University Press.
Conklin, Harold
1957 Hanunoo Agriculture. Rome: Food and Agriculture Organization of the United Nations.
Coyett, Frederick
1975 Neglected Formosa: A Translation from the Dutch of Frederic Coyette's 't Verwaerloosde Formosa. Inez de Beauclair, ed. San Francisco: Chinese Materials Center.
Crocker, J. Christopher
1979 Selves and Alters among the Eastern Bororo. In Dialectical Societies: The Ge and Bororo of Central Brazil. David Maybury-Lewis, ed. Pp. 249–300. Cambridge, MA: Harvard University Press.
Dahrendorf, Ralf
1968 Essays in the Theory of Society. Stanford, CA: Stanford University Press.
Davison, Julian, and Vinson Sutlive
1991 The Children of Nising: Images of Headhunting and Male Sexuality in Iban Ritual and Oral Literature. In Female and Male in Borneo. Vinson Sutlive and George N. Appell, eds. Pp. 153–230. Borneo Research Council Monograph Series, 1. Shanghai, Virginia: Ashley Printing.
Devereux, George
1976[1955] A Study of Abortion in Primitive Societies. New York: International Universities Press.
Divale, William
1984 Matrilocal Residence in Pre-Literate Society. Ann Arbor, MI: UMI Research Press.
Divale, William, and Marvin Harris
1976 Population, Warfare, and the Male Supremacist Complex. American Anthropologist 78:521–538.
Douglas, Mary
1969 Is Matriliny Doomed in Africa? In Man in Africa. Mary Douglas and Phyllis Kaberry, eds. Pp. 121–135. London: Tavistock.
Dozier, Edward P.
1966 Mountain Arbiters. Tucson: University of Arizona Press.
Dunn, Halbert L., comp.
1949 Vital Statistics of the United States, 1947, Part I. Washington, DC: U.S. Public Health Service.
Eaton, Joseph W., and Albert J. Mayer
1954 Man's Capacity to Reproduce: The Demography of a Unique Population. Glencoe, IL: Free Press.
Eggan, Fred
1950 Social Organization of the Western Pueblos. Chicago: University of Chicago Press.

1954 Social Anthropology and the Method of Controlled Comparison. American Anthropologist 56:743–763.

Ember, Melvin, and Carol Ember

1971 The Conditions Favoring Matrilocal versus Patrilocal Residence. American Anthropologist 73:571–594.

Endicott, K. M.

1970 An Analysis of Malay Magic. London: Oxford University Press.

Evans, Ivor H. N.

1953 The Religion of the Tempasuk Dusuns of North Borneo. Cambridge, England: Cambridge University Press.

Evans-Pritchard, E. E.

1951 Kinship and Marriage among the Nuer. Oxford: Oxford University Press.

Ferrell, Raleigh

1969 Taiwan Aboriginal Groups: Problems in Cultural and Linguistic Classification. Institute of Ethnology Monograph, 17. Taipei: Institute of Ethnology, Academia Sinica.

1971 Aboriginal Peoples of the Southwestern Taiwan Plain. Bulletin of the Institute of Ethnology, Academia Sinica 32:217–235.

Firth, Raymond

1967 Tikopia Ritual and Belief. London: George Allen and Unwin.

Fischer, David H.

1970 Historians' Fallacies: Toward a Logic of Historical Thought. New York: Harper and Row.

Floud, Roderick, Kenneth Wachter, and Annabel Gregory

1990 Height, Health and History: Nutritional Status in the United Kingdom, 1750–1980. Cambridge, England: Cambridge University Press.

Fock, Niels

1967 South American Birth Customs in Theory and Practice. *In* Cross-cultural Approaches. Clellan S. Ford, ed. Pp. 126–144. New Haven, CT: HRAF Press.

Foley, Frederic J.

1968 The Great Formosan Impostor. St. Louis, MO: Jesuit Historical Institute, St. Louis University. Reprinted, Taipei: Mei Ya.

Fortes, Meyer

1970 Time and Social Structure: An Ashanti Case Study. *In* Time and Social Structure. Pp. 1–32. London: Athlone.

Fox, Robin

1967 Kinship and Marriage. Harmondsworth: Pelican Books.

Freeman, Derek

1970 Report on the Iban. New York: Humanities Press.

1979 Severed Heads That Germinate. *In* Fantasy and Symbol. R. H. Hook, ed. Pp. 233–246. New York: Academic Press.

Freud, Sigmund

1977[1925] Some Psychical Consequences of the Anatomical Distinction between the Sexes. *In* On Sexuality: Three Essays on the Theory of Sexuality and Other Works. Pp. 331–343. Harmondsworth: Penguin Books.

1950 Totem and Taboo: Some Points of Agreement between the Mental Lives of Savages and Neurotics. James Strachey, trans. New York: W. W. Norton & Company.

Fuller, C. J.
  1976 The Nayars Today. Cambridge, England: Cambridge University Press.
Gallen, Moira
  1982 Abortion in the Philippines: A Study of Clients and Practitioners. Studies in Family Planning 13(2) (February):35–44.
Garvan, John M.
  1929 The Manobos of Mindanao. Memoirs of the National Academy of Sciences, 23(1). Washington, DC: National Academy of Sciences.
Gordon, Linda
  1976 Woman's Body, Woman's Right: A Social History of Birth Control in America. New York: Grossman Publishers.
Gough, Kathleen
  1961 Variation in Residence. *In* Matrilineal Kinship. David Schneider and Kathleen Gough, eds. Pp. 545–576. Berkeley: University of California Press.
Gross, Daniel R.
  1979 A New Approach to Central Brazilian Social Organization. *In* Brazil: Anthropological Perspectives. Maxine L. Margolis and William E. Carter, eds. Pp. 321–342. New York: Columbia University Press.
Grothe, J. A.
  1886 Archief voor de Geschiedenis der Oude Hollandsche Zending III: Formosa 1628–1643. Utrecht: C. Van Bentum.
Grove, Robert D., and Alice M. Hetzel
  1968 Vital Statistics Rates in the United States, 1940–1960. Washington, DC: U.S. Dept. of Health, Education and Welfare.
Hall, Calvin S.
  1954 A Primer of Freudian Psychology. New York: Mentor Books.
Halpern, Joel
  1958 A Serbian Village. New York: Columbia University Press.
Hanson, F. Allan
  1982 Female Pollution in Polynesia? The Journal of the Polynesian Society 91(3):335–381.
Hanson, Jeffery R.
  1988 Age-set Theory and Plains Indian Age-grading: A Critical Review and Revision. American Ethnologist 15(2):349–364.
Hart, Donn V.
  1965 From Pregnancy through Birth in a Bisayan Filipino Village. *In* Southeast Asian Birth Customs. Donn V. Hart et al., eds. Pp. 1–113. New Haven, CT: HRAF Press.
Hempel, Carl G.
  1965 The Logic of Functional Analysis. *In* Aspects of Scientific Explanation. Pp. 297–330. New York: Free Press.
Ho T'ing-jui
  1956a P'ing-tung hsien Lai-i hsiang P'ai-wan tsu chih wen shen yü lieh t'ou [Tattooing and Headhunting of the Chalaabus Paiwan]. Bulletin of the Department of Archaeology and Anthropology [National Taiwan University] 6:47–49.
  1956b T'ai-ya tsu lieh t'ou feng su chih yen chiu [A Study of Atayal Headhunting Customs]. Wen shih che hsueh pao 7:151–208.
Holy, Ladislav, and Milan Stuchlik
  1983 Actions, Norms, and Representations: Foundations of Anthropological Inquiry. Cambridge, England: Cambridge University Press.

Horton, Robin
  1983 Social Psychologies: African and Western. *In* Oedipus and Job in West
        African Religion. Meyer Fortes, ed. Pp. 41–87. Cambridge, England: Cam-
        bridge University Press.
Hose, Charles, and William McDougall
  1912 The Pagan Tribes of Borneo, Volume 2. London: MacMillan and Com-
        pany.
Hoskins, Janet
  1988 Matriarchy and Diarchy: Indonesian Variations on the Domestication
        of the Savage Woman. *In* Myths of Matriarchy Reconsidered. Deborah
        Gewertz, ed. Pp. 34–56. Oceania Monographs. Sydney: University of Syd-
        ney Press.
Howell, Nancy
  1979 The Demography of the Dobe !Kung. New York: Academic Press.
Hsieh Shih-chung
  1987 Jen t'ung ti wu ming: T'ai-wan yüan chu min ti tsu ch'ün pien ch'ien
        [Stigmatized Identity: Ethnic Change among Taiwan Aborigines]. Taipei,
        Taiwan: Tzu li wan pao she.
Huang Hsuan-wei (Huang Shiun-wey)
  1988 I-wan A-mei-tsu ch'uan-t'ung sui-shih chi-i ti fen-hsi [An Analysis of
        the Traditional Calendric Rituals of the I-wan Ami]. Unpublished manu-
        script.
Hunt, Edward E., Nathaniel R. Kidder, David Schneider, and William D.
Stevens
  1949 The Micronesians of Yap and Their Depopulation. Cambridge, MA:
        Peabody Museum, Harvard University.
Hunt, Edward E., Nathaniel R. Kidder, and David M. Schneider
  1954 The Depopulation of Yap. Human Biology 26(2):21–51.
Huntington, Richard, and Peter Metcalf
  1979 Celebrations of Death. Cambridge, England: Cambridge University
        Press.
International Fertility Research Program
  1981 Traditional Abortion Practices. Research Triangle Park, NC: Interna-
        tional Fertility Research Program.
Ishii Masao
  1990 Childbirth and Gender in Central Sulawesi. *In* Kinship, Gender, and the
        Cosmic World: Ethnographies of Birth Customs in Taiwan, the Philippines,
        and Indonesia. Yamaji Katsuhiko, ed. Pp. 187–211. Taipei, Taiwan: SMC
        Publishing.
Jenks, Albert E.
  1905 The Bontoc Igorot. Manila: Bureau of Public Printing.
Kapferer, Bruce
  1988 The Anthropologist as Hero: Three Exponents of Post-Modernist An-
        thropology. Critique of Anthropology 8:77–104.
Kasahara Masaharu
  1986 Childbirth Customs among the Puyuma. *In* Childbirth and Childrear-
        ing in Western Oceania. Goda Toh, ed. Pp. 39–54. Kobe: Kobe University
        College of Liberal Arts.
Keesing, Felix
  1962 The Ethnohistory of Northern Luzon. Stanford, CA: Stanford Univer-
        sity Press.

Keesing, Roger
   1982 Introduction. *In* Rituals of Manhood. Gilbert H. Herdt, ed. Pp. 1–43. Berkeley: University of California Press.
Kennedy, Robert E., Jr.
   1973 The Irish: Emigration, Marriage, and Fertility. Berkeley: University of California Press.
Kim Kwang-ok
   1980 The Taruko and Their Belief System. Ph.D. dissertation, Oxford University.
King, Victor
   1976 Transition and Maloh Birth. Folk 18:189–204.
Kirch, Patrick V.
   1984 The Evolution of the Polynesian Chiefdoms. Cambridge, England: Cambridge University Press.
Kloos, Peter
   1963 Matrilocal Residence and Local Endogamy: Environmental Knowledge or Leadership. American Anthropologist 65(4):854–862.
Kuepers, J. J. A. M.
   1978 The Dutch Reformed Church in Formosa, 1627–1662: Mission in a Colonial Context. Immensee, Switzerland: Nouvelle Revue de Science Missionaire.
Lach, Donald, and Edwin Van Kley
   1993 Asia in the Making of Europe, Volume 3, A Century of Advance, Book Four, East Asia. Chicago: University of Chicago Press.
Laderman, Carol
   1983 Wives and Midwives: Childbirth and Nutrition in Rural Malaysia. Berkeley: University of California Press.
Lambrecht, Francis
   1938 The Mayawyaw Ritual III: Death and Death Ritual. Publications of the Catholic Anthropological Conference 4(3):327–493.
Lave, Jean
   1979 Cycles and Trends in Krikati Naming Practices. *In* Dialectical Societies: The Ge and Bororo of Central Brazil. David Maybury-Lewis, ed. Pp. 16–45. Cambridge, MA: Harvard University Press.
Leach, E. R.
   1958 Magical Hair. The Journal of the Royal Anthropological Institute 80(2):147–164.
Lee, Lois
   1972 Pregnancy and Childbirth Practices of the Northern Roglai. Southeast Asia 2(1):26–52.
Lévi-Strauss, Claude
   1969 The Elementary Structures of Kinship. Boston: Beacon Press.
Li Yi-yuan
   1982[1957] Nan-shih A-mei tsu ti pu lo tsu chih [The Tribal Organization of the Nan-shih Ami]. *In* T'ai-wan t'u chu min tsu ti she hui wen hua. Pp. 139–78. Taipei, Taiwan: Lien-ching ch'u pan shih yeh kung ssu. (Reprinted from the Bulletin of the Institute of Ethnology, Academia Sinica, volume 4.)
Liu Pin-hsiung
   1965 Hsiu-ku-luan A-mei tsu ti she hui tsu chih [Social Structure of the Hsiu-ku-luan Ami]. Institute of Ethnology Monograph, 8. Taipei, Taiwan: Institute of Ethnology, Academia Sinica.

1969 Sha-a-lu-a tsu ti she hui tsu chih [Social Structure of the Saaroa]. Bulletin of the Institute of Ethnology, Academia Sinica 28:67–158.

Lloyd, P. C.
1965 The Yoruba of Nigeria. *In* Peoples of Africa. James L. Gibbs, ed. Pp. 547–582. New York: Holt, Rinehart and Winston.

Lunn, Peter G.
1991 Nutrition, Immunity, and Infection. *In* The Decline of Mortality in Europe. Roger Schofield, D. Reher, and A. Bideau, eds. Pp. 131–145. Oxford: Clarendon Press.

Mabuchi Toichi
1960 The Aboriginal Peoples of Formosa. *In* Social Structure in Southeast Asia. George P. Murdock, ed. Pp. 127–140. Chicago: Quadrangle Books.
1974 Ethnology of the Southwestern Pacific. Taipei, Taiwan: Orient Cultural Service.

MacFarlane, Alan
1986 Marriage and Love in England, 1300–1840. Oxford: Basil Blackwell.

Malthus, T. R.
1989[1803] An Essay on the Principle of Population, Volume 1. Patricia James, ed. Cambridge, England: Cambridge University Press.

Martin, Emily
1988 Gender and Ideological Differences in Representations of Life and Death. *In* Death Ritual in Late Imperial and Modern China. James L. Watson and Evelyn S. Rawski, eds. Pp. 164–179. Berkeley: University of California Press.

Matsuzawa Emiko
1986 The Paiwan Social System and Its Impact on Childbirth. *In* Childbirth and Childrearing in Western Oceania. Goda Toh, ed. Pp. 1–25. Kobe: Kobe University College of Liberal Arts.

Maybury-Lewis, David
1967 Akwe-Shavante Society. Oxford: Oxford University Press.
1979a Cultural Categories of the Central Ge. *In* Dialectical Societies: The Ge and Bororo of Central Brazil. David Maybury-Lewis, ed. Pp. 218–246. Cambridge, MA: Harvard University Press.
1979b Conclusion: Kinship, Ideology, and Culture. *In* Dialectical Societies: The Ge and Bororo of Central Brazil. David Maybury-Lewis, ed. Pp. 301–312. Cambridge, MA: Harvard University Press.

Meillassoux, Claude
1981 Maidens, Meal and Money: Capitalism and the Domestic Community. Cambridge, England: Cambridge University Press.

Merquior, J. G.
1985 Foucault. Berkeley: University of California Press.

Metcalf, Peter
1982 A Borneo Journey into Death: Berawan Eschatology from Its Rituals. Philadelphia: University of Pennsylvania Press.

Miyamoto, Masaru
1988 The Hanunoo-Mangyan. Osaka, Japan: National Museum of Ethnology.

Miyauchi Etsuzo
1940 Iwayuru Taiwan Banzoku no Shintai Henko [Body Deformations of Taiwan Aborigines]. Jinruigaku senshigaku koza 19:1–45.

Montesquieu, Baron de
  1758 The Spirit of the Laws. M. Nugent, trans. London: Nourse and Vaillant.
Morokvasic, Mirjana
  1984 Sexuality and Control of Procreation. *In* Of Marriage and the Market.
    Kate Young et al., eds. Pp. 193–209. London: Routledge & Kegan Paul.
Murdock, George P.
  1949 Social Structure. New York: MacMillan Company.
  1959 Africa: Its Peoples and Their Culture History. New York: McGraw Hill.
Murphy, Robert F.
  1960 Headhunters' Heritage. Berkeley: University of California Press.
Myers, W. W.
  1884 Notes on the Aborigines of South Formosa. Customs Medical Reports
    28:39–46. Shanghai: Inspectorate-general of Customs.
Nakamura Takashi
  1936 Ranjin jidai no bansha kako hyo [The Dutch Period Aborigine Census
    (1650)]. Nanpo dozoku 4:42–59.
  1937 Ranjin jidai no bansha koko hyo, 2 [The Dutch Period Aborigine Census,
    Part 2 (1655)]. Nanpo dozoku 4:182–196.
  1959 Shih ch'i shih chi T'ai-wan lu p'i chih ch'u ch'an chi ch'i tui Jih mao i
    [The Production of Deerskins in Seventeenth-century Taiwan and Their
    Trade to Japan]. T'ai-wan yen chiu ts'ung k'an 71:24–42.
Narkavonnakit, Tongplaew, and Tony Bennett
  1981 Health Consequences of Induced Abortion in Rural Northeast Thai-
    land. Studies in Family Planning 12(2):58–65.
Nash, Jill
  1968 A Note on Groomprice. American Anthropologist 80:106–108.
Needham, Rodney
  1985 Psalmanaazaar, Confidence-man. *In* Exemplars. Pp. 75–116. Berkeley:
    University of California Press.
Obeyesekere, Gananath
  1981 Medusa's Hair. Chicago: University of Chicago Press.
Ogawa Masayasu
  1990 Symbolic Implications of the Tsou House. *In* Kinship, Gender, and the
    Cosmic World: Ethnographies of Birth Customs in Taiwan, the Philippines
    and Indonesia. Yamaji Katsuhiko, ed. Pp. 77–101. Taipei, Taiwan: SMC
    Publishing.
Okada Yuzuru
  1942 Mikai Shakai ni okeru Kazoku [The Family in Primitive Society]. Tokyo:
    Kobundo.
O'Meara, J. Tim
  1989 Anthropology As Empirical Science. American Anthropologist 91:354–
    369.
Ortner, Sherry
  1981 Gender and Sexuality in Hierarchical Societies: The Case of Polynesia
    and Some Comparative Implications. *In* Sexual Meanings. Sherry B. Ortner
    and Harriet Whitehead, eds. Pp. 359–409. Cambridge, England: Cambridge
    University Press.
Paige, Karen, and Jeffrey Paige
  1981 The Politics of Reproductive Ritual. Berkeley: University of California
    Press.

Pedrosa, Ramon
   1983 Abortion and Infanticide in the Philippines during Spanish Contact.
      Philippiniana Sacra 18(52):7–37.
Peletz, Michael G.
   1987 The Exchange of Men in 19th-Century Negeri Sembilan (Malaya).
      American Ethnologist 14(3):449–469.
Potts, Malcolm, Peter Diggury, and John Peel
   1977 Abortion. Cambridge, England: Cambridge University Press.
Psalmanaazaar, George
   1926[1704] An Historical and Geographical Description of Formosa: An
      Island Subject to the Emperor of Japan. The Library of Impostors, 2. N. M.
      Penzer, ed. London: Robert Holden & Company.
Quirino, Carlos, and Mauro Garcia
   1958 The Manners, Customs, and Beliefs of the Philippine Inhabitants of
      Long Ago; Being Chapters of "A Late 16th Century Manila Manuscript,"
      Transcribed, Translated and Annotated. The Philippine Journal of Science
      87(4):325–453.
Reid, Anthony
   1988 Southeast Asia in the Age of Commerce 1450–1680, Volume One, The
      Lands below the Winds. New Haven, CT: Yale University Press.
Reid, Lawrence A.
   1972 Wards and Working Groups in Guinaang, Bontoc, Luzon. Anthropos
      67:530–563.
Richards, A. I.
   1950 Some Types of Family Structure amongst the Central Bantu. *In* African
      Systems of Kinship and Marriage. A. R. Radcliffe-Brown and Daryll Forde,
      eds. Pp. 207–251. London: Oxford University Press.
Ritter, Madeline L.
   1980 The Conditions Favoring Age-set Organization. Journal of Anthropo-
      logical Research 36(1):87–104.
Riviere, Peter
   1984 Individual and Society in Guiana: A Comparative Study of Amerindian
      Social Organization. Cambridge, England: Cambridge University Press.
Rosaldo, Michelle Z., and Jane M. Atkinson
   1975 Man the Hunter and Woman. *In* The Interpretation of Symbolism. Roy
      Willis, ed. Pp. 43–75. London: Malaby Press.
Roth, Eric A.
   1993 A Reexamination of Rendille Population Regulation. American Anthro-
      pologist 95(3):597–611.
Roth, H. Ling
   1893 On the Signification of Couvade. Journal of the Anthropological Insti-
      tute of Great Britain and Ireland 22:204–243.
Rutter, Owen
   1929 The Pagans of North Borneo. London: Hutchinson.
Sahlins, Marshall
   1972 Stone Age Economics. New York: Aldine.
   1976 Culture and Practical Reason. Chicago: University of Chicago Press.
Sather, Clifford
   1978 The Malevolent *Koklir:* Iban Concepts of Sexual Peril and the Dangers
      of Childbirth. Bijdragen tot de taal-, land-en volkenkunde 134:310–355.

St. John, Spenser
  1863 Life in the Forests of the Far East. 2 vols. London: Smith, Elder & Company.
Sayama Yukichi
  1914 Banzoku chosa hokokusho: A-bi zoku kimitsu sha [Survey Reports on the Formosan Aborigines: The Ami of Chi-mi she]. Tokyo: Rinji Taiwan Kyukan Chosakai dai ichibu [The Temporary Commission for the Investigation of Traditional Customs in Taiwan, First Department].
Scharer, Hans
  1963 Ngaju Religion. The Hague: Martinus Nijhoff.
Schlegel, Alice
  1972 Male Dominance and Female Autonomy: Domestic Authority in Matrilineal Societies. New Haven, CT: HRAF Press.
Schlegel, Stuart A.
  1979 Tiruray Subsistence: From Shifting Cultivation to Plow Agriculture. Quezon City, Philippines: Ateneo de Manila University Press.
Schneider, David
  1961 The Distinctive Features of Matrilineal Descent Groups. *In* Matrilineal Kinship. David Schneider and Kathleen Gough, eds. Pp. 1–29. Berkeley: University of California Press.
  1968 Abortion and Depopulation on a Pacific Island. *In* Peoples and Cultures of the Pacific. Andrew P. Vayda, ed. Pp. 383–406. New York: The Natural History Press.
Schroder, Dominik
  1967 The Puyuma of Katipol (Taiwan) and Their Religion. Bulletin of the Department of Archaeology and Anthropology [National Taiwan University] 29–30:11–59.
Scott, William H.
  1975 German Travelers on the Cordillera, 1860–1890. Manila: Filipiniana Book Guild.
Shapiro, Judith
  1987 Men in Groups: A Reexamination of Patriliny in Lowland South America. *In* Gender and Kinship: Essays Toward a Unified Analysis. Jane F. Collier and Sylvia J. Yanagisako, eds. Pp. 301–323. Stanford, CA: Stanford University Press.
Shepherd, John R.
  1986 Sinicized Siraya Worship of A-li-tsu. Bulletin of the Institute of Ethnology, Academia Sinica 58:1–81.
  1993 Statecraft and Political Economy on the Taiwan Frontier, 1600–1800. Stanford, CA: Stanford University Press.
Shih Chuan-kang
  1993 The Yongning Moso. Ph.D. Dissertation, Stanford University.
Shih Lei
  1971 Fa-wan: I ke P'ai-wan tsu pu lo ti min tsu hsueh t'ien yeh tiao ch'a pao kao [Su-Paiwan: An Anthropological Investigation of a Paiwan Village]. Institute of Ethnology Monograph, 21. Taipei, Taiwan: Institute of Ethnology, Academia Sinica.
Skeat, Walter W.
  1900 Malay Magic. London: MacMillan and Company.

Stockard, Janice
  1989 Daughters of the Canton Delta. Stanford, CA: Stanford University
    Press.
Tambiah, S. J.
  1970 Buddhism and the Spirit Cults in North-east Thailand. Cambridge,
    England: Cambridge University Press.
  1973 The Form and Meaning of Magical Acts. *In* Modes of Thought. Robin
    Horton and R. Finnegan, eds. Pp. 199–229. London: Faber and Faber.
T'ang Mei-chun
  1973 A Structural Analysis of the Burial Customs and Funeral Rites of Lai-i,
    An Aboriginal Village in Taiwan. Bulletin of the Department of Archaeol-
    ogy and Anthropology [National Taiwan University] 33–34:9–34.
Tanner, Nancy
  1974 Matrifocality in Indonesia and Africa and among Black Americans. *In*
    Woman, Culture, and Society. Michelle Z. Rosaldo and L. Lamphere, eds.
    Pp. 129–156. Stanford, CA: Stanford University Press.
Taussig, Frederick J.
  1936 Abortion: Spontaneous and Induced. St. Louis: C. V. Mosby Co.
Thompson, Laurence
  1964 The Earliest Chinese Eyewitness Accounts of the Formosan Aborigines.
    Monumenta Serica 23:163–204.
Ting Hung-hsueh
  1978 Hsiu-ku-luan A-mei tsu ti nung li yü nung ye chi ssu, I [The Agricultural
    Calendar and Agricultural Rituals of the Hsiu-ku-luan Ami, I]. T'ai-wan jen
    wen 3:72–87.
Tsuchida Shigeru
  1988 Taiwan Takasagozoku shago ni okeru 'kushami' to kinki [Sneezing and
    Taboo in the Taiwan Aboriginal Languages]. Tokyo daigaku gengogaku
    ronshu 1988:21–34.
Turner, Terence
  1979a The Ge and Bororo Societies as Dialectical Systems: A General Model.
    In Dialectical Societies: The Ge and Bororo of Central Brazil. David May-
    bury-Lewis, ed. Pp. 147–178. Cambridge, MA: Harvard University Press.
  1979b Kinship, Household, and Community Structure among the Kayapo.
    In Dialectical Societies: The Ge and Bororo of Central Brazil. David May-
    bury-Lewis, ed. Pp. 179–214. Cambridge, MA: Harvard University Press.
  1980 The Second Skin. *In* Not Work Alone. J. Cherfas and R. Lewin, eds. Pp.
    112–140. Beverly Hills: Sage.
Underwood, Jane H.
  1973 The Demography of a Myth: Abortion in Yap. Human Biology in
    Oceania 2(2):115–127.
Valeri, Valerio
  1990 Both Nature and Culture: Reflections on Menstrual and Parturitional
    Taboos in Huaulu (Seram). *In* Power & Difference: Gender in Island South-
    east Asia. Jane M. Atkinson and S. Errington, eds. Pp. 235–272. Stanford,
    CA: Stanford University Press.
Wang Jen-ying
  1967 T'ai-wan Kao-shan tsu ti jen k'ou pien ch'ien [Population Change of
    Formosan Aborigines]. Institute of Ethnology Monograph, 11. Taipei: Insti-
    tute of Ethnology, Academia Sinica.

Wang Sung-hsing

1961 Ma-t'ai-an A-mei tsu chih tsung chiao chi shen hua [Religion and Myth among the Vataan Ami]. Bulletin of the Institute of Ethnology, Academia Sinica 12:107–178.

1964 Taiwan Sirayazoku no shakai soshiki [The Social Organization of the Siraya of Taiwan]. Minzokugaku Kenkyu 29(2):168–172.

Wei Hui-lin, Yü Chin-chüan, and Lin Heng-li

1952 Ts'ao tsu p'ien [Ethnography of the Tsou]. *In* T'ai-wan sheng t'ung chih kao, Volume 8, t'ung chou chih, part 1. Taipei: T'ai-wan Sheng wen hsien wei yüan hui.

Westermarck, Edvard A.

1922 The History of Human Marriage, Volume 3. New York: Allerton Book Co.

Wolf, Arthur P.

1986 The Meaning of "Marriage." Bulletin of the Institute of Ethnology, Academia Sinica 59:19–27.

Wolf, Margery

1972 Women and the Family in Rural Taiwan. Stanford, CA: Stanford University Press.

Wolff, Robert J., R. DeSanna, and J.-P. Chaine

1971 A Study of Knowledge, Attitude and Practice of Contraception in the Trust Territory of the Pacific Islands, 1970. Honolulu: International Health, Population and Family Programs, School of Public Health, University of Hawaii.

Wright, David

1671 Notes on Formosa. *In* Atlas Chinensis. Arnoldus Montanus, ed. Pp. 17–37. John Ogilby, trans. London: T. Johnson. Reprinted in Shepherd 1986:56–76.

Wrong, Dennis H.

1961 The Oversocialized Conception of Man in Modern Sociology. American Sociological Review 26(2):183–193.

Wu Yen-ho (David)

1965 P'ai-wan tsu tung P'ai-wan ch'ün ti wu yi yü wu shu [Shamanic Curing and Magical Arts among the Eastern Paiwan]. Bulletin of the Institute of Ethnology, Academia Sinica 20:105–154.

Yamaji Katsuhiko

1990 Female Activity in the Amis of Taiwan. *In* Kinship, Gender, and the Cosmic World: Ethnographies of Birth Customs in Taiwan, the Philippines and Indonesia. Yamaji Katsuhiko, ed. Pp. 49–75. Taipei, Taiwan: SMC Publishing.

Yu, Elena, and William T. Liu

1980 Fertility and Kinship in the Philippines. Notre Dame, IN: University of Notre Dame Press.

Yuan Chang-rue

1969 Ta-kang-k'ou ti A-mei tsu [The Makutaai Ami of Eastern Taiwan: An Ethnographic Report]. Institute of Ethnology Monograph, 18. Taipei: Institute of Ethnology, Academia Sinica.

Breinigsville, PA USA
23 November 2009
228041BV00002B/3/P